SO YOUR FOOT'S
IN THE DOOR ...
NOW WHAT?

SO YOUR FOOT'S IN THE DOOR

NOW WHAT?

Steven J. Schwartz

Fitzhenry & Whiteside
Toronto

In the United States,
121 Harvard Avenue, Suite 2, Allston, Massachusetts 02134

www.fitzhenry.ca   godwit@fitzhenry.ca

Fitzhenry & Whiteside acknowledges with thanks the Canada Council for the
Arts, the Government of Canada through the Book Publishing Industry
Development Program (BPIDP), the Ontario Arts Council and the Government
of Ontario through the Ontario Media Development Corporation's Ontario
Book Initiative for their support for our publishing program.

10 9 8 7 6 5 4 3 2 1

National Library of Canada Cataloguing in Publication

Schwartz, Steven J., 1956-
So your foot's in the door... now what? : how to create the environment
where people want to buy / Steven J. Schwartz.

ISBN 1-55005-058-3

1. Selling. I. Title.

HF5438.25.S34 2003   658.85   C2003-900588-7

U.S. Publisher Cataloging-in-Publication Data
(Library of Congress Standards)

Schwartz, Steven J.
So your foot's in the door ... now what? : how to create the environment
where people want to buy / by Steven J. Schwartz. – 1st ed.
[192] p. : cm.
Summary: Provides salespeople with tools needed to persuade,
influence and close sales swiftly, effectively and with style.
ISBN 1-55005-058-3 (pbk.)
1. Salesmen and salesmanship. 2. Selling. I. Title.
658.85 21   HF5438.S39 2003

Design: *Mad Dog Design Connection*
Printed and bound in Canada

Dedicated to everyone I have the privilege of coaching. Thanks for elevating my methods and inspiring those around you with your success.

Contents

Introduction

Chances are you are not the only person making sales calls on your prospective customer. If you and your competitor are walking in the door offering something of equal value, how you treat the customer can make all the difference, and this begins with how the sale is made. I'm not going to reinvent the sales process; the essential elements of selling remain unchanged in this book. I can, however, enhance your ability to persuade, influence and close with the kind of personal selling behaviors that create the environment where people want to do business with you. This is important not just for those occasions when you call on customers, but also when they call on you, as they do at retail sales or trade shows, for instance. I will also help you to be more effective in your sales calls by providing you with Islands of Structure in an otherwise unstructured environment, so that you can better control the direction and outcome of your face-to-face encounters. I even go the extra mile by giving you a very detailed process for creating, rehearsing and testing the content of your presentations.

For years, many salespeople have used manipulative language to secure a quick transaction with a customer they would never see again; the kind of behavior that people have come to expect from sales. That's one reason why some people don't like selling, and why others are stressed out thinking about how they are going to close their next deal. If you are not comfortable trying to sell someone something they don't really need or want, imagine how the customer must feel!

My system is based on respect: respect for you, your customers and the sales call itself; the kind of respect that builds lasting relationships that nurture future business and referrals. *You won't have to worry about closing when you create the environment to close.*

This book developed from conversations I had with numerous people who profited from reading my previous bestseller, *How To Make Hot Cold Calls*, which provided a proven system for reaching and influencing decision makers. Now that I have helped them get in the door, my readers expressed a strong need for being more effective at closing more sales, and so this sequel was born. That said, let me assure you the book you have in your hands is very much a stand-alone methodology, and you don't need to have read my previous work to benefit from this one. To make it easy for you to implement the material, this book is "hands-on." It walks you through the "how to's," applying all the tools and processes you'll need.

Like my previous methods, this approach is based on my own experience as one who has been self-employed for almost a quarter-century, and one who has tested this approach in the school of hard knocks. I have simply taken what was intuitive and wrapped it in a process that anybody can use successfully. Providing you with a system gives you the very two things you need to reach your objectives: consistency and predictability. You can't have predictability without consistency, and you can't have consistency without a system. Most important, this system enables you to quickly raise your performance benchmarks by giving you the ability to self-assess after each sales call, eliminating mistakes and building your own best practices.

People across North America whom I have trained on this system have sent me feedback on what you can expect from it, other than the obvious increase in sales. Here's what they said in their own words:

- "It definitely helps accelerate the buy decision and shortens the sales cycle."
- "It helps you effectively lay out objectives and content for presentations."
- "You will get more of the information you need to qualify and close the business."
- "Meetings will be more structured."
- "You and your audience will be more focused."
- "Less time per sales call."
- "Customers will more likely want to have a relationship with you."
- "You won't leave anything to chance."
- "Meetings are in a logical order so that people can follow you."
- "Uncovers roadblocks to success."
- "You will keep people with you every step of the way."
- "The structure gives you a purpose going in and enables you to know if you meet your objectives going out."

It's what *you* have to say that counts. So join me as we walk through a proven system that is easy to read, easy to apply, and easy to buy into. Now that you have your foot in the door, it's time to create the environment where people want to buy...from you!

The Fundamentals

This system is based on principles that are referenced throughout this book. They were established because—being the Virgo that I am—I was compelled to analyze the prerequisites for success in the face-to-face sales call, and in the process discovered these truths, which make perfect sense. I'm sure you'll agree.

Have To vs. Want To

Unless you have a monopoly, people don't buy from you because they have to. They buy because they want to. So your job is to make sure that your customers are in a WANT TO frame of mind. People WANT TO do business with you for a variety of reasons; they like you, they have a clear need or desire for your product or service, and perhaps what you offer is unique, unusual or leading edge. Whatever the reasons, it's important not to take a prospective customer for granted. This goes double when you are selling to an existing customer. How many times have you ever received a call from a company you do business with and the salesperson automatically assumes that you are going to sit there and listen to that person pitch a new product or service?

I have an expression: "no one wakes up in the morning looking for your product, unless you are selling coffee." Whether you are meeting with customers or prospective customers, always respect the fact that people don't have to buy from you, and in fact, they don't even have to give you the time of day for this meeting or any other. The challenge is to create an atmosphere where they WANT TO. That's plenty to think about.

Understand and Relate

People have to UNDERSTAND and RELATE to your message in order to act. These are two different issues. If you want me to UNDERSTAND what you are saying, you will have to speak my language. So for example, if I was a technical guy and you were selling software, by all means be technical. But if I was not gifted in the ways of technology, don't use the technical jargon on me because you'll lose me. Speak in plain terms. Any time jargon is used there is the potential to alienate your audience.

If you want people to RELATE to what you are saying, you would have to give them examples or explain your offering in a way that fits the world of your audience. For example, suppose you want to sell me wireless e-mail.

How would you communicate your message so that I could RELATE to it? You could score points by drawing an analogy around the frustration I'm having with my current e-messaging:

> "Steven", you begin, "have you ever sent messages to colleagues who travel a lot?"
> "All the time," I concur.
> "How do you feel when they are out of town and you need to get some vital information to them immediately?" you continue.
> "Frustrated. It happens all the time," I add.
> "Then imagine how you would feel if you could get that information to your associates no matter where they are, because they won't need to be tied to a phone line."
> "I can do that? Let's talk!"

Now I not only UNDERSTAND, I RELATE to your example and therefore I am in a position to act.

Now here's the challenge: very often people won't tell you that they don't UNDERSTAND or RELATE to what you are talking about. (Some people find it embarrassing to admit that they don't UNDERSTAND something, and would rather nod politely as your meeting goes on.) That's the silent killer of deals. You never know what hit you. In short, you experience a sudden, silent disconnect from your audience. This is precisely why this whole system is centered on how to stay connected with your audience throughout the entire sales cycle. All it takes is one disconnect and you are toast. So stay close with me on this one.

The power to connect with customers accelerates the buy decision.

Creating an environment to close

All your efforts are leading up to a single moment when
your prospect or customer is going to take action, whatever action happens to be required. Closing the deal should
not under any circumstances be manipulative or forced.
This whole system is designed to create an environment to
close, one where you are in control and connected with
your audience. Many top producers will tell you that when
you create an environment that is conducive to making a
purchase, people are more likely to buy from you.

You have an audience

When I was in my youth I paid my way through university as a professional sleight-of-hand artist performing magic
at trade shows, nightclubs and in television commercials.
When I went out to establish my own business in advertising at age twenty-three, I used my performing acumen
in my sales calls. It gave me an edge over professional
account executives, who had many more years of sales
experience than I did. My performing background made
me instinctively UNDERSTAND that I was not so much
addressing a customer or prospective customer or the VP
of marketing for that matter, but that I was speaking
before an audience. You are too. That's why throughout
this book I am often going to refer to your prospects and
customers as your audience.

When people think of an audience they tend to think
of many people crowded together in a room. However,
any time you speak or present to someone—even if it's
with just one person—you have an audience. When you
have an audience you are giving a performance. I'm not
suggesting that your sales calls be artificial, or even that
you have to be a professional actor. But thinking in terms

of an audience will change the way you view your position. Picture yourself standing in front of a customer, and tell me what you see. There is a customer and there is you, who happens to be either a salesperson or consultant. Now picture yourself standing before an audience. Who is that performer on center stage? That's right. It's you! That's an entirely different responsibility. When you are giving a performance you control the audience and not the other way around.

You keep people listening through the power of your words and the passion with which they are spoken.

You have to constantly read an audience and know what they are thinking even when they are not speaking. An audience has to be moved emotionally. An audience is to be respected. An audience, after all, is mobile. They can leave at any time. It's up to you to make sure they WANT TO stay and listen to your every word.

Perhaps the biggest impact an audience has on your way of thinking is this: any great performance is planned, rehearsed, tested and perfected. Your sales call should be too.

Islands of Structure

Your challenge of staying connected with your audience is made all the more interesting because the face-to-face sales call is by its very nature an unstructured environment; you can't control what people will say, do or ask. So how do you maintain control over your sales call? The answer lies in creating Islands of Structure in an unstructured environment.

Islands of Structure are specific moments when you take control of your sales call and, as a result, control the outcome.

There are ten islands of structure:

1. First impressions
2. Turning your audience on
3. Tuning your audience in
4. Taking the reins
5. Reading the audience
6. Verifying
7. Offering the solution
8. Closing
9. Testing
10. Presentations

Each one of these "Islands" is simple to execute, yet the real power here lies in the fact that they are all joined together in a sequence that creates the successful environment to close.

Imagine you had twenty extension cords all plugged into one another, with the last one plugged into your power source. If only one extension cord is disconnected, you won't get any power. It's the same with these Islands of Structure. You leave one out, you lose control and disconnect from your audience. Together they power your sale.

Islands Of Structure

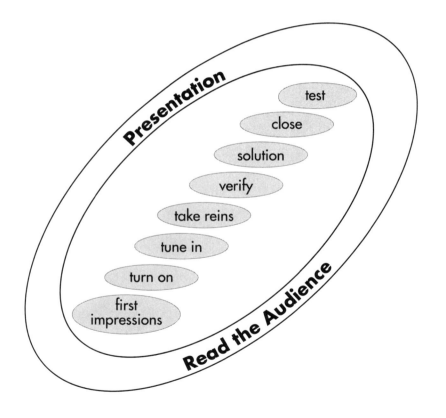

Island 1
First Impressions

A good first impression is the first step to connecting with your audience. People buy from people they like, and that positive feeling begins with first impressions. You actually have two opportunities to make a first impression, one on the phone in your initial telephone sales call and the other when you first meet in person. If you did not make a good impression on your telephone sales call, you won't have a face-to-face sales call to concern yourself with.

First impressions are lasting impressions, and here's why: you move in the direction of the images you create and your audience will move in the direction of the images you create. That's why we're going to address the two first impressions you need to focus on: the impressions you create in your own mind before your sales call and the impression you first make on your audience during your sales call.

Your own first impression of the sales call

If you can see yourself building a business chances are you will, but if you can't see yourself running a company, chances are you won't. It's the same with your sales. If you can't see yourself making a sale, how will your customers envision the purchase?

So before you even walk into a sales call make sure you have the right image in your mind. You have to see yourself acquiring and handling the business. It has to be real to you. I have come across all kinds of people who confided in me that there were many occasions when they did not pursue a profitable opportunity simply because it was larger than what they had handled in the past. As a result they lacked the confidence to go after it.

If you are self-employed you'll relate to this. Do you remember your first $1,000 contract? Once you were used to getting these $1,000 orders the next milestone was your first $5,000 contract. Wasn't the first $10,000 order an even bigger thrill? But what was it like going after your first $30,000 deal? $50,000 deal? A lot of people tell me the $100,000 sale is a big milestone, and only after you have delivered on a few of those do you feel confident that you can close a $1-million deal. Part of what goes through your mind at each of these milestones is a process of either doubting or confirming your worthiness for such an amount. Some psychologists say that by age three each of us has a subconscious limit of success that we feel worthy of, and if later in our career we approach that place, the stress increases because we have no comfort level going beyond it. We have no image in our mind that says such a thing can or should happen. (That is one reason why many incredibly successful people subconsciously sabotage their success just when they seem to be reaching the top.)

The same can happen when you are applying for a job or a higher position with greater authority. You might want that promotion to VP level, but unless you can see it and taste it and be comfortable with it, it won't be yours.

As you get to the next level in the size of your sales orders, I want you to think of this increase as an accomplishment that you have earned, through hard work no less. Each accomplishment is a milestone to reward. A reward can be something you want to do, something you want to buy, somewhere you want to go or time off work. For example, here's a simple reward schedule you can customize:

Milestone	*Reward*
$1,000 sale	
$5,000 sale	
$10,000 sale	
$30,000 sale	
$50,000 sale	
$100,000 sale	
$500,000 sale	
$1,000,000 sale	

Each time you reward yourself you will be focused on the next reward, and in doing so the milestones will look after themselves.

Now, even if you feel worthy of the business, are you comfortable handling the business? Unless you are confident in your ability to deliver on the business you are pursuing, your subconscious just might look for ways to make sure your sales call is not a successful one. This happens to lots of people. Once someone commits to hiring you, or purchasing a large order, you have to be able to deliver.

To help you feel confident about taking on a bigger

sale, here's a checklist of prerequisites that must be in place in order for you to keep your commitments:

❒ Time
❒ Tools
❒ Skills
❒ Knowledge
❒ Resources
❒ Authority

If you are missing just one of these prerequisites for success, you may have difficulty delivering on the order. With all in place, you should be confident that you can take on the job.

I remember that for the first five years of my career I deliberately went looking for creative challenges that I knew were over my head, but I had the confidence that I would rise to the occasion. To me, growth was not just in terms of dollars and accounts but knowledge and skill. The way I saw it, the tougher the assignments I took on, the smarter I would become and the more marketable too since others would seek me out to perform similar challenges. But if I didn't have the confidence to go over my head, the growth in my career would never have happened.

Aside from feeling good about taking on the opportunity you are pursuing, you also need to feel comfortable with the size of the audience you are addressing. I remember the first time I presented in front of a hundred people, and how nervous I was before, just thinking of it. After doing it successfully I moved on to speaking in front of two hundred people and then five hundred. At one point I reached the milestone of speaking in front of over a thousand people, and after that experience an audience of a few hundred seemed quaint. Each time I reached a new milestone I had to visualize the audience so I could mentally prepare myself for the next milestone. (We'll talk more about preparation in the Presentation section.) I'm sharing this with you to illustrate the impact the size of your audience can have on your ability to perform successfully, and to point out that you need to take the time to mentally prepare yourself for speaking in front of an audience that is larger than the last.

Even if there is only one other person in the room with you, you have to be confident when conversing, especially when that person is in a higher position. For example, it's not uncommon for people to feel hesitant about speaking to CEOs and CFOs of corporations. (When you speak with people in these positions, keep your conversation focused on their issues and what's important to them.) One technique I learned when I was in my early twenties to overcome this hesitation was to visualize that I was calling peer to peer. After all, I too was the president of a company—my own—even if it was only a company of one.

Your Audience's First Impression

The very first impression you make actually takes place at the beginning of the customer relationship, which is your initial telephone sales call. Whether you are calling on a prospect, or someone is calling you from a referral, the reality is that whatever you say the first time you speak will leave your prospect with a certain impression of you, which will be carried forward to your first meeting. Every word you speak on the phone paints an image in someone's mind, and yes, you have control over what those images are. Your tone also conveys a message, such as your professionalism and your love of what you do. If you come across like you are trying to sell something, you'll have an uphill battle, not just for your initial sales calls, but also for years to come, because every time you visit your customers they will never trust your intentions or advice completely. But if you come across as simply sharing an opportunity, and you talk about what's important to your customers (rather than what's important to you), then you will have an easier time earning that trust and moving your sales cycle forward. If you read How To Make Hot Cold Calls you have already learned the methodology on how to portray the right image on that first call.

I strongly believe that after people form an opinion of you on the phone, they spend your first meeting subconsciously justifying their initial impression of you. Hold that thought: I have to tell you a funny story here.

When I was in my twenties starting my own business, I looked like I was eighteen (I guess I had a bit of a baby face). But to counter this, I always came across on the phone like I was in my forties because I spoke with a lot of confidence. The funny thing was that after having booked an appointment to see a prospective customer, there I was sitting in the reception area flanked with other, older salespeople who were in their thirties, forties and fifties, also waiting to go into their sales calls. Without fail, the prospect would walk up to one of them and say, "Mr. Schwartz, it's nice to see you." You can imagine the look on the prospect's face when I raised my hand and said with a smile, "I'm Mr. Schwartz."

Your Second First Impression

Your second first impression takes place in the first ten minutes of your initial face-to-face sales encounter. People rightly or wrongly judge you at first by what you look like, what you wear, and the chemistry between you. Their opinion of you will later be shaped by what you say, what you do, and what you know.

Impressions Based on Appearance

Dress to suit your audience, but also dress for success. When I was an advertising writer and creative director I wore jeans and stylish Italian sweaters. Everyone else on the creative team wore the same, replete with cowboy boots. We looked creative because that's what we were expected to be. We weren't expected to wear suits; that was left to the "suits," better known as account executives.

These days I always ask in advance what the dress code is for the companies I visit. You might not wish to show up in a suit with everyone else dressed in business casual. It might make some people feel uncomfortable. If I am unable to find out what the dress code is, I prefer to go a little over-dressed, rather than underdressed for the occasion.

Dress is especially critical when you are in the fashion business. I once went shopping to buy a pair of shoes. When the shoe salesman came up to me and said, "May I help you?" I glanced down and noticed that the shoes he was wearing were unpolished and worn out. I took a pass, thank you. If that's the respect the fellow has for the products he represents, how can I value his opinion?

It's hard to measure how your outward appearance affects the outcome, but one thing is for certain: your appearance creates an image and you need to make sure that it is the image you want to portray.

Impressions Based on Chemistry

Chemistry is one of those magical intangibles that connects people. Part of the chemistry comes from sharing a common background, culture or interests. (The second Island of Structure will show you how to connect on areas of mutual interest.) Chemistry also comes from the energy you exude because people are attracted to energy. Some of that comes from your natural disposition while other energy is a product of your enthusiasm. The most basic energy comes from exercise and plenty of rest. If you know that you have a big presentation tomorrow, get a good night sleep. Food is also a factor. Various reactions to foods can affect your performance. For example, I notice that red wine makes me a little sluggish in the morning so I avoid wine if I have a meeting to go to the next day.

Don't skip your lunch.

"But Steven, who has time for lunch these days?"

I know. I know. But what's your objective? Energy. Your body is a machine and that machine gets its energy from food. Watch out for carbohydrates; pasta and potatoes can make you drowsy.

I'm always amazed at how people will spend millions of dollars on technology to drive productivity gains, and yet go out and have a few alcoholic drinks at lunch. So much for productivity. To stay focused and energized, take note of what you are putting into your system.

If you have to make a presentation in the afternoon, don't be afraid to put your head down for a ten-minute nap after lunch. I think that North Americans are about the only people in the world who don't practice this natural energy booster. This is especially important for "morning people" who find that they have all the energy in the morning yet fade in the afternoon. These people must be careful about making sales calls at 2 p.m., which is the time when their body clocks requires rest, the time when morning people are least productive. So if you are one of them, as am I, either take that power nap or schedule your presentation after 3 p.m.

Exercise is also important.

Actually, I'm going to stop here for a minute to make sure you're still with me. I don't want you to think I'm off on a tangent with all this talk about getting enough sleep and eating right and exercising. This stuff is really important. It keeps your energy level up, and energy plays a big role in the impression you make. It really is that important. Now where was I…. exercising.

I'm not about to suggest you need a fitness program. But even a thirty-minute walk a day is going to help here. Walking is good for lowering stress so your mind is clear and can focus on the job at hand. You always focus best when your energy is up.

Impressions Based on How You Speak

When you are articulate and speak with confidence you build trust for one simple reason: people believe you know what you're talking about. I'm not just talking about avoiding slang and bad grammar. I'm referring as well to your ability to speak with clarity. Communicate what you have to say so that the listeners clearly UNDERSTAND your meaning. Prepare effective answers to the most asked questions to give your audience the clarity of meaning they are looking for. Know your products, services and subject matter inside out so you can stand behind everything you say.

And when you say it with passion, the world is yours. People that exude energy are also people who are passionate about what they do. Your love of what you do or your love of meeting people creates natural energy and a tone that shows you're enthusiastic. Anyone who sounds passionate about life tends to draw others around them. If you love your work and you believe in what you are selling, it shows. When I first started out with a threadbare portfolio, the one thing that endeared me to my clients was my passion. It was clear to all that I loved what I did and believed in what I created. I haven't changed.

The energy, commitment and passion that you bring to your job are the emotional investments in your work. Do you put your heart and soul into your job? When you have an emotional investment in what you are offering, you believe with all your being that you are improving the lives of your customers. When you believe that strongly in the value you bring to the table you will exude the kind of passion that motivates people to WANT TO do business with you.

Passion is the fashion.

If you are having an off day you can instantly turn on your passion by focusing on all the good things your customers have said about you in the past, or by taking a moment to simply reflect on all the ways you have helped your customers. Let's take a moment to top off your emotional investment.

What do you love about your work or the people you work with?

. . . .
. . . .

What was the last nice thing a customer said to you?

. . . .
. . . .

What is the best way you add value for your customers?

. . . .
. . . .

The next time you go out to a restaurant, ask the waiter to

recommend a dish on the menu. Forget what he says. Tune in to how he says it. If your waiter sounds blasé, take a pass. If he gets all excited and raves about a particular entrée, go for it. I do this all the time and I've found the waiters to be right over ninety per cent of the time when they're passionate about the food they are talking about.

One summer day I was passing by an ice cream place with a friend. When asked which flavor was best, the women behind the ice cream counter pointed to the chocolate and said with a huge smile on her face, "It's to die for!" My resistance broke down completely. And was she right. So listen for passion, and understand that is what others are listening for too.

Impressions Based on Your Actions

Many years ago I was expecting a knock at the door from an insurance agent who was referred to me. This fellow, who was new to the business, was coming to my home to talk about disability insurance, which I highly recommend to anyone who is self-employed. But I digress.

Knock. Knock.

As soon as I open the door, and before the agent even steps foot in my home, he says "Nice home you have." My home was nice, but how could he tell? The guy hasn't even seen it yet. So my first impression is that he is insincere and as such cannot be fully trusted. Since trust is the basis of any relationship, it's not hard to figure out where this relationship is headed.

I have a suspicion that this fellow is here to sell me anything he can, regardless of whether it is in my best interest. The only reason I give him a second chance to prove himself is because he comes referred. He does his fact-finding routine, and then gets back to me later that week to tell me that he has to see me again to get some more information. After a few visits, he sends me a contract to sign for what he claims is the best policy I can get. Right. Normally I would have left it at that and signed, but that gnawing bad first impression makes me wonder if I should hold off until I have a second opinion.

The night before the insurance agent is to come by for the contract I ask a friend at a party to tell me who his insurance agent is. "You didn't sign the contract already?" he asks. "No," I reply, at which point I am given the name of another agent. I call up the first fellow and tell him to hold off for a few days. I contact the new referral, and lo and behold, I get a very different first impression. This fellow Charles asks me all kinds of questions on the phone, really trying to get an understanding of what I need. He then says that he will see me the next day after he does his homework and works out exactly what policy is best for me.

I hang up the phone thinking, "this fellow is doing his homework," my kind of guy. The fact that he was doing the work upfront demonstrates a level of professionalism and a healthy respect for my time. Charles shows up and instead of spending time with chitchat or fact-finding, he already has my options fully laid out and explains them in great detail. He really did do his homework. It ends up that the policy he offers provides double the coverage of what the first agent proposed, and at less cost, plus it is a policy that is worded specifically to cover the liabilities of writers (like not being able to use my hands).

The contract is signed without delay.

Impressions Based on Your Product Knowledge

Here's a classic Schwartz pet peeve: how many times have you walked into a store and asked the sales people a question only to get the reply, "I don't know." Worse, they don't find out. You almost have a desire to tell them that this isn't a contest. You are not quizzing them for the fun of it. You need the information in order to make a purchase! A salesperson is supposed to make it easier for you to make that purchase. That's why it is every salesperson's job to know everything about what they are selling. A few months ago I went into a real estate office at a new executive home development. I asked the salesperson if the kitchen cupboards contained any particleboard or if they were solid wood. The fellow had no clue. If you are selling a $700,000 home you should know your product. If you are selling a $20 product, you should also know it inside out.

Your ability to effectively answer any questions goes beyond looking credible and establishing trust. People need answers to their questions in order to make a buying decision. Providing good answers is also just plain good service. If people are not going to take the time to answer your questions, why would you believe they will take the time to help you after the purchase? You are also doing a disservice to your customers because some of them who really could benefit from your products or services will walk away unable to make the very purchase which they clearly need. I'm sure you have been angry on occasions where you wanted to make a purchase but walked away without the information you needed, and months later you got that information when it was too late to buy the product and you thought to yourself, "I wish they would have told me when I asked. I would have bought it!"

If you are working for a company that has many products or services and you simply do not have the time to learn every detail about all the offerings, the good news is that you don't have to know everything. Granted, the more you know the better, especially if that knowledge comes from having used the products yourself so that you can speak from personal experience. But knowing every last piece of information is not a prerequisite for having a meaningful conversation. To find the essential information you need to know, put on your thinking cap and answer the following questions:

What are the main questions people ask about your product/service?

. . . .
. . . .
. . . .
. . . .

What will people need to know about your product/service in order to make a buying decision?

. . . .
. . . .
. . . .
. . . .

How do people use your product/service?

. . . .
. . . .
. . . .

Have you used your own product/service for similar purposes? If so, what was your personal experience with the product? What sort of questions did you have about it? Was it easy to use?

. . . .
. . . .

. . . .
. . . .

Is there anything complicated about using your product
or service that requires an explanation or demonstration
of some kind?

. . . .
. . . .
. . . .
. . . .

What is unique about your product or service?

. . . .
. . . .
. . . .

How much does your product or service cost, and why is
it worth the price?

. . . .
. . . .
. . . .
. . . .

Two days ago I went to two different manufacturers of
espresso machines. The first place I visited had two models I was interested in, one more expensive than the other.
The salesperson was not able to explain what I was getting for the difference in price. (I don't mind paying more
for something as long as I can see the value.) When I visited the second manufacturer, I saw two other models—

one was $300 more than the other. Only this time the salesperson talked at great length about the unique qualities of the more expensive model; the way it was manufactured, the features that made it easier to make a perfect espresso (he demonstrated many of those features), and the design elements that made cleaning and maintenance easier. Perhaps because of his knowledge he spoke passionately about the machine. His passion and product knowledge made me trust his opinion and made it possible for me to actually make a buying decision.

Now, the people you are planning to visit on your next sales call will want to make decisions as well. The good first impression you create will get you to the point where you can sit down and start a meaningful discussion. You might be energetic and passionate, but what about your audience? It's time to get them turned on too.

Island 2
Turn Your Audience On

All good performers will tell you that some of the best performances they have given were ones where the audience was full of energy. When people are energized they are alert and focused on what you're talking about. However, you never know in what state you'll find the people in your sales call. For instance, they might not be morning people and your 8:30 meeting is catching them in a tired state of mind. They might be coming into the meeting distracted with other issues. You have to take control here to make sure that their energy and attention is where you need it. Imagine that your audience has an "on" switch in their minds and all you have to do to get their energy flowing is turn it on.

When you are meeting people for the first time, one of the most effective ways to "turn your audience on" is to tap into something they are passionate about. When you tap into passion you bring out positive feelings and tons of energy. You also create a special bond or chemistry between you and your prospect, because for a few moments—at least—you are sharing a common experience, and one that you both feel strongly about. Your shared experience will give you an instant connection which will help set you apart from everyone else, and most important, make your prospect WANT TO hear what you have to say.

Let's look at how to quickly identify and leverage what your audience is passionate about.

Identifying the Passion Points

The moment someone takes you into their office, look around at your surroundings. Specifically, look for clues that tell you what sort of hobbies or sports the person is into, or anything that looks like it's a one-of-a-kind item. These clues might be found on their desk or on the walls, or they might be part of the furnishings. When you spot them, ask yourself which ones you too have an affinity towards.

For example, someone's photos might reveal that this person has won a golf trophy. That desk might be an antique. The walls might be filled with degrees from the same university you graduated from. The paintings on the wall might be originals (signaling an interest in art), or all the same subject matter, such as landscape paintings (demonstrating an interest in nature).

Leveraging the Passion Points

As soon as you identify an area of common interest, like an antique desk, don't jump on it right away. You have to look nonchalant. Wait until you sit down and then point to the desk and drop a comment ever so casually such as, "I love your antique desk. I go antique hunting every chance I get." What you did was reference their passion and then let it be known that you share the same passion. It's very important to reference your own interest; otherwise it might just come out as a compliment. If you were to simply say, "I love your antique desk," the person might take it as a passing nicety and either say nothing at all or reply briefly with a remark like, "I've had it for years." But when you remark that you too go antique hunting, you will cement a bond and have a greater chance of opening the dialogue on a deeper level! You can also drop the first part where you identify their passion ("I love your antique desk") and go straight to your passion, "I go antique hunting every chance I get." It sounds even more compelling and can sound like you are sharing something from the heart. Chances are your prospect will respond with something like, "So do I! Where do you go? What period do you look for?"

When someone opens up, watch his or her body language. People can get quite animated and energetic and sometimes go on for quite some time talking about antiques—where they buy them, their best purchases, what they're on the hunt for now and so on.

Be prepared for the fact that you might not see signs of things you have in common, or even if you do and drop the hint, some people may not respond at all. In either event don't worry about it. Just get on with the business at hand. If they pick up the bait, it's a bonus. A big bonus.

I remember meeting a VP of training at one of the large brokerage houses. This rather reserved, stern-faced fellow named Jim greets me in the reception area, offers a few words of idle chitchat ("Hope you weren't waiting too long") and then escorts me to his office. No sooner do I enter than I notice a coffee table book on his desk called

Equus Reined by Robert Vavra, which has the most breathtaking pictures of horses you will ever see. As luck would have it, not only do I have the same book, but I also have a passion for riding horses, which I was willing to bet Jim did too.

As I was walking toward the chair he was escorting me to, I pointed to the book on the way and then ever so casually said, "I have the exact same book. I ride horses in the Rockies every summer." I thought it would be fun to mention that I shared both his book and his passion for the subject matter. Mr. Reserved instantly turned into Mr. Animated. "You do!" he said with his arms up in the air. "Where do you ride?" Without skipping a beat we spent the next forty-five minutes talking about nothing else but horses. The next half-hour after that was spent on business, but by then we had bonded so well that he wanted to do business with me before we even talked shop.

This kind of engagement happens all the time. Sure, there are occasions where someone doesn't pick up on the cue, but these are few and far between. Whether people do or don't, or whether they talk for only a minute or for hours about the passion you share, you only have an upside. Where else can you get better odds than that?

When you are networking at a function or a party, here's a fast way to bring out the passion. Instead of asking "What do you do?" ask, "What do you do for fun?" Watch how people get animated.

Once you get people turned on, you have created an environment where people WANT TO listen to what you have to say. To get their instant undivided attention all you have to do is tune your audience in to the subject at hand, much like you would adjust the dial on your radio to the program you want to listen to.

Island 3
Tune Your Audience In

After you have been given a coffee and asked to sit down, it's time to get down to business. You don't want to sit there for an hour with the small talk—and believe me, that can happen, especially if you are meeting people who are not overly busy at the time and want to appear busy by spending time in meetings. You need to be the one who takes control and gets the ball rolling. If you have an opportunity to turn your audience on you will probably be talking for a few minutes about whatever passions you have in common. If there was no opportunity to have that kind of discussion, you will be ready to begin the meeting.

You have the power to set the direction, tone, atmosphere and success of your meeting.

You do what's right at the beginning of the meeting by simply establishing the agenda. If your meeting was arranged through a telephone sales call, the purpose of your visit has already been established. But very often someone's spouse or business partner shows up and that person only has second-hand information as to why you are there. As well, some priorities may have changed since the appointment was booked, and your prospect may have other things to talk to you about.

Getting people tuned in to what needs to be discussed gets the conversation moving in the right direction and helps focus their thoughts. Your agenda should reiterate the main reason why your audience should invest the time to listen to what you have to say. Remember, they don't HAVE TO listen to you, so why would they WANT TO?

How to Set the Agenda

If you have not met your prospect before, as soon as you want the meeting to commence, reiterate exactly what you said on the phone when you booked the appointment. (If you need an effective process for creating your telephone script, review the scripting section in *How To Make Hot Cold Calls*.) After all, if what you said captured enough interest to land the appointment, it should be leveraged to get your prospect tuned in.

Suppose on the phone you said, "Good morning Mr. Schwartz, we've never been introduced before, my name is John Reader. And I'm calling because I have a lot of experience helping companies reduce advertising costs by up to twenty per cent and access lucrative markets that are not affordable by conventional media. I was wondering when we could meet to discuss your advertising strategy and the new market opportunities we can introduce you to."

When you are seated at the meeting you just arranged, you would set the agenda by saying, "I'm here today because I have a lot of experience helping companies reduce advertising costs by up to twenty per cent and access lucrative markets that are not affordable by conventional media." Since you just said something your audience wants to hear and you addressed an issue that was top of mind, it's bound to get them tuned in and deliver their undivided attention. I refer to this as hitting the Greed Glands; they're tucked away somewhere in the back of the brain, and light up every time people hear about a solution to a pressing problem, or a mention of something they are looking for or urgently need. Greed Glands are triggered whenever someone's ears hear an answer to the question, "What's in it for me?" The more effectively you reach those Greed Glands, the more people will WANT TO listen to what you have to say and will be more willing to openly share their true situation with you.

At this point you would proceed to ask some qualifying questions to open up the conversation, which you'll learn more of in our next Island of Structure. What you have accomplished by using this technique is getting your audience focused on why they need to listen further. A lot of people tell me that this technique also helps them pull focus, because they know what they're going to say at the beginning of the meeting and won't be at a loss for words.

Setting the agenda also gives people an opportunity to confirm the agenda—because it's your agenda on the table. A client of mine named Bruce walked into a sales call only to discover that the agenda had changed. It seems that the company was now dealing with some new business issues that had not surfaced when Bruce made his original call. That was fine with Bruce, who was able to recalibrate and talk about how he could help address the new challenges the company was facing. Imagine what would have happened if Bruce had not set the agenda and instead had proceeded to talk about the original agenda, which the prospect was no longer interested in. The meeting would have gone nowhere fast. Instead he was able to capture a new opportunity in real time.

If you are meeting with people for a second time, set the agenda by reiterating what you had agreed to discuss when you left your previous appointment with them. For example, you can say, "When we last spoke we had agreed that I would come back and..."

With your agenda firmly established and agreed to, where do you go from here? It's time to take the reins and set your conversation off in the right direction.

Island 4
Taking The Reins

All my years of riding horses in the Rockies have taught me that it's one thing to get a horse moving, and quite another to gently steer it along to where you have to go. That's what Taking the Reins is all about. It's a way to get the dialogue moving forward after you set the agenda and then keep your audience clearly focused on where you are going. How many times have you been on a sales call where people started talking about things that were not relevant to your conversation, and as a result, the whole meeting got sidetracked and blown off course? One would be one too many, but we've all been there. When a meeting goes in the wrong direction you end up not getting the information you need to move on to the next step.

Even though you cannot ultimately control what people are saying, you can control the direction of the conversation and the kind of information you receive by framing the conversation at the beginning. The way to do this is to qualify your audience by asking three main questions, which we'll get to in a minute. You qualify your prospect right away for two reasons: the first is that you need to know as soon as possible if there is a basis for a sale here. If someone doesn't have a need for your product or service, you have nothing to sell, in which case why waste everyone's time? (Some of that qualifying may have already taken place on the phone during your telephone sales call.) The second reason is more profound: selling is either something that is done to you or it helps you make a buying decision.

Too often sales has received a reputation as something that is "done to people" because too many people were trying to sell other people something they didn't need or want. Repeat customers don't come out of such relationships. Products and services are only a means to an end. If the end is not articulated and agreed to, you will sound like you are selling (forcing the sale on others) instead of sharing an opportunity and helping them make a buying decision. If a salesperson came up to you and said, "Mr. Reader, I'd like to talk to you about a software program that automates all your weekly bookkeeping functions," how would you react if bookkeeping were not discussed as a problem? You'd be thinking, "This person is pushing the bookkeeping software of the week on me and he doesn't really care if I need it or not."

Unfortunately a lot of people rush right into talking about their products and services before anyone has articulated a need for anything. These salespeople only end up sounding like they're trying to push something on someone and often have an uphill battle in closing, which is why closing often becomes a manipulative act (which it never should be).

You create an environment to close when you find out what people need and then offer it to them. While there are dozens of questions you will probably need to ask throughout the course of your various discussions with your prospective customers, I discovered that the best place to start is by asking the three most essential questions that will open the door to the other qualifying questions. These three questions can be asked at any time: over the phone when you are calling a prospect; over the phone when a referral calls you and you need to quickly take control of the conversation; at the beginning of a meeting right after you set the agenda; and right before you present your product or service. These three key questions also keep you in control in those situations where customers often just drop by and you never know what they want to discuss.

I call these three essential qualifying questions Control Questions because they keep you in control of the sales call. In this sense they are sort of like a compass. You can't get lost in the conversation or blown off track because you will always know the direction your conversation needs to be headed, namely moving from one Control Question to another.

Control Questions will help you and your audience better UNDERSTAND the needs at hand, and help your audience RELATE to your solution because the conversation will be centered on their own experience. Let your audience have all the time they need to fully answer your questions. Do more listening than talking.

Give your audience a chance to tell their story before you tell yours.

Control Questions fall into these categories:

Control Question 1: Lay of the Land
Control Question 2: Frame the Pain
Control Question 3: What's at Stake

Lay of the Land

When you first meet someone, the first question you ask is designed to give you the Lay of the Land. It shows you how your prospect is currently set up for doing business. You could be looking for how many locations the company has, the kinds of suppliers it has, where it ships its products, how it markets, etc. This might sound like Elementary Qualifying 101, but it needs to be done consistently.

Finding out the Lay of the Land gives you a clear picture of the environment in which your offerings might be applied. If you were an architect designing a custom home, I suppose you could design it without ever seeing the landscape in which it was being placed. But if you did take the time to visit the future site of the home, you would alter your design plans to accommodate the scenery; you might adjust the kitchen to capture the morning light, or add bay windows to capture a view of a forest. These additions would also be up-selling opportunities for you, which would be easy to offer the customer. Instead of asking homebuyers if they would like a kitchen solarium, you could simply ask if they would appreciate the opportunity to have breakfast with the morning light pouring in the kitchen? Sounds appealing, doesn't it?

When I'm scouting the Lay of the Land, the first qualifying question I ask is, "What are you currently doing to open new doors of opportunity?" From there my prospect will tell me about how they bring in sales: VARS, distributors, direct sales force, call centers, and whatever direct marketing is done in support of their telemarketing activities. This information tells me how my training program will fit into their sales strategy, which is important because I train a direct sales force differently than a call center team. It also alerts me to issues which my experience tells me they are likely to have; issues that they sometimes are not even aware of. The bottom line is that the Lay of the Land information I receive enables me to tailor my future questions more specifically, and discuss an appropriate solution more intelligently.

For instance, if people tell me that they have a direct sales force, I'm going to ask them about compensation to see if there are any roadblocks to performance. If the answer comes back that the sales force is solely paid by commissions it will alert me to an interesting problem: people on pure commission tend to be overanxious in their sales calls which leads to fewer appointments. I will therefore likely recommend a specific reward and recognition program to remedy this situation.

If people tell me that they rely heavily on telemarketing from their corporate call centers, I will need to find out if the call centers are taking inbound or outbound calls, which not only effects the way my solution is delivered, but also alerts me to other concerns we may need to discuss such as employee motivation. If my prospect does not have a corporate call center and instead is using an outside service bureau, then I know to talk about issues of control since companies in this situation have less control over the way their corporate image is portrayed to their customer base.

The information my prospects give me can also reveal gaps in their strategy which will present more opportunities for me. For example, they may need a direct marketing campaign to support their telemarketing efforts, or require additional training for their direct sales force that will be handed leads from the call center.

Here's another quick example of a Lay of the Land-type question. If you were in the transportation business you might ask a potential customer a question like, "What markets are you currently shipping to?" The answer you get shows you which service offerings you should discuss, how competitive you will be for their business (you might be cost-effective in certain markets), and if you learn that there are some markets that are not being exploited, you can ask why. You might learn that someone isn't shipping a certain distance because it's not cost-effective with the current supplier, but what the individual did not know was that you are cost-effective in that area. You end up with a new business opportunity just for having asked the right question. Your prospect might even tell you about areas into which they are about to expand where no one had bid on the transportation side of the business.

As you can see, by asking the initial Lay of the Land question you can uncover needs, discover potential roadblocks to implementing your solutions, shed light on new opportunities you might not be aware of, and you can add a sense of urgency for further qualifying questions.

If you are having a second or third meeting with someone, check if the landscape has changed, especially if it's been a while since you last saw him or her. A question like, "What's changed since the last time we spoke?" will do nicely. This is also true if you are calling on a company you are already doing business with. Things change and companies don't always tell their suppliers everything, especially when mergers are about to happen or someone is leaving.

So never assume that you know everything. Ask the questions. I recently had a client in the transportation business that called on a company he knew very well. While my client Mike had not actually done any business with this firm before, he thought he knew all the markets

this company was shipping to. Nevertheless, he took nothing for granted and in his first meeting asked the question,
"Where are you currently shipping?" To my client's surprise, and utter delight, he found out that this company
had northbound business out of the U.S. which he was not
previously aware of. Mike went on to bid on the business
and secured a contract worth $100,000 a year. Not bad for
asking a question.

Frame the Pain

As you know, you cannot sell something to someone without first understanding what the person needs. I mentioned before that some of those needs will reveal
themselves as you learn the Lay of the Land. The rest has
to come from a more detailed probe. People generally
need something without having a problem associated
with that need, or they have a specific problem in search
of a solution.

For example, suppose you are working in a hardware
store and a couple comes up to you and asks your advice
on which car-wash soap they should buy. They probably
don't have a problem; they just want to clean their car and
can't decide which product is better. Well, the better one
is the one that best addresses their need. As a good salesperson you would ask the customers a question such as,
"How often do you wash your car?" or, "Do you leave your
car out of the garage at night?" If they wash their car often,
then you would offer the larger size because it's more economical. If they leave the car out of the garage and
exposed to the elements, you might suggest they purchase
some wax as well to protect the shine (not that I was
deliberately leading you to an up-sell opportunity here).

Most often when you are knocking on a door in the

business world, the people you are seeing have more than just a need; they have a problem or business issue that needs to be addressed. I refer to this need as their "pain" because it's a need that has to be cured. Even if you know what your prospect's problems are, or where the pain is, you may not be aware of how complex the problem is or what other factors are contributing to the issue. Internal events you are not privy to might be creating issues you will need to learn about. Don't make any assumptions. Find out from the source.

When you ask a question to Frame the Pain, listen to the answer very, very carefully. It is important not just to hear what the problem is, but also to get your prospects to express the pain in their own words because by doing so, the pain becomes real. When people articulate problems the words pass from their lips to their ears, and then to their minds, where the words create images. Those images can also conjure up lots of emotions. When someone feels the pain emotionally there is a greater sense of urgency to get rid of the pain. (Who wants pain?) When feelings come to the surface you also tend to have a more energetic, passionate discussion. You might notice a change in body language; people lean toward you, stand up, move their arms, or just sound more passionate. The more animated your audience becomes, chances are the more acute the pain.

Now is probably a good time to give you an example of a Frame the Pain kind of question. Let's suppose you are a real estate agent.

You: (Lay of the Land): "What part of the house do you use most?"

Me: "The kitchen but the deck is a close second."

You: (Frame the Pain): "If you could change anything at all about your kitchen, what would it be?"

Me: "I need more counter space. I do a lot of entertain-
      ing and there is never enough room to prepare
      everything all at once. I constantly have to make
      one or two courses at a time and then clean every-
      thing up to free some space so I can start on the
      next course. Come to think of it, I could use a larg-
      er eating area as well so I have some room to lay out
      the appetizers for my larger dinner parties."

Notice how the Lay of the Land question got you
focused on the kitchen, while the Frame the Pain probing
revealed that counter space was the deeper need, all of
which presented you with a very clear selling opportunity. Since counter space is important to your customer, it's
now important to you, and all the homes you will show
will be ones with lots of counter space. If these homes
should also happen to have a large eating area, you'll probably seal the deal.

One other reason why your audience has to articulate
their pain is that even though a real problem or challenge
exists, the prospect might be in denial and not recognize
the problem. How many companies have you seen go
under because they never addressed issues that were eating away at the profitability of their business? If you don't
hear a problem, it doesn't mean there isn't one. It just
means you might need to dig further and ask more
questions.

This is where you can leverage your experience. The
more you know of an industry or the marketplace you are
dealing with, the more you can anticipate the kind of
issues your audience may be facing. This knowledge will
help you ask more questions so you can get at the real
issues. This will be most helpful when your prospects are
not sure what problems they are facing (there might be
more than one) or they have difficulty in articulating them.

But you need to get those needs on the table just the same.

For example, when I visit executives to talk about how they can build top producers, and after they have answered my Lay of the Land question ("What are you currently doing to open new doors of opportunity?"), I Frame the Pain with this question: "What are the challenges you face in opening those doors?" One day a VP answered this question by saying he wanted his people to be able to book appointments with seventy per cent of the decision makers they call. My experience had taught me that the real problem might not be in their ability to book appointments. Rather, the problem might be that they were not able to get these executives on the phone to have a conversation with them in the first place. I knew I had to drill down further, so I asked, "If your salespeople called twenty decision makers, how many would they actually speak with?" The answer came back that they only reached three out of twenty, which meant that they were missing eighty-five percent of their opportunities. That was a significant issue worth addressing, and one I could easily remedy.

Here's another example. If you were an insurance agent and wanted to uncover my needs or expectations, you could ask a question as simple as, "What do you want your insurance to do for you?" At that point your prospective customer will tell you what her concerns or needs are. It might be to protect her income, save for retirement or any number of needs that will be as different as the individual herself. On the other hand some people might not know the answer, so you might want to talk about what you do for others.

As your experience grows, keep a database or list of the most important issues each company or industry segment is facing. The idea is to keep this list with you in your meetings so you can quickly know which qualifying ques-

tions to ask in order to uncover hidden needs that for
whatever reason are not being expressed. Try a simple
grid like this:

Industry	Issues	Symptoms
. . . .		
. . . .		
. . . .		

Think for a moment about the next sales call you are
about to make. Dig into your experience and give some
thought to the following:

What are the most common issues/challenges
companies like this face?

. . . .
. . . .

What are the outward signs to look for that tell
you these problems exist?

. . . .
. . . .

What other issues are often associated with these
problems?

. . . .
. . . .

What are some possible solutions?

. . . .
. . . .

Whether those outward signs and issues surface on their
own in your meeting or you have to probe to see if your cus-

tomer has experienced them, once they are confirmed you will know the precise challenges which need to be addressed (whether the customer was aware of them or not).

If after you Frame the Pain you discover that someone has no issues at all, then you can't very well offer a solution. (That's why it's a good idea to qualify people on the phone beforehand, if you can.) I had a situation once where I secured an appointment with a VP of sales at a large media company to talk about helping his salespeople become more efficient and effective at booking appointments with decision makers. Phil the VP of sales brought along his VP of training. When I asked him, "What are the challenges you are facing in opening new doors of opportunity?" he replied—and I kid you not—"We don't have any challenges." Now, you and I both know that this was not the case or else he would not have arranged the meeting with me in the first place. Whether he was testing me or trying to play some power game I don't know, but I wasn't interested in playing. So what did I do? Without a moment's hesitation I smiled, closed my laptop computer, and as I placed it in my briefcase I said, "If you have no challenges there is nothing for me to offer you in the way of assistance." At this point he looked stunned. As I headed for the door he jumped out of his chair and quickly said, "Wait! Wait! We have some challenges. Please sit down." I did. He got honest with himself and opened up to the issues of the day. While my actions were not done to earn his respect (although I'm sure they did), I did what I did because I'm serious when I say that without a real need there is no basis for a sale.

When people across the desk answer your Frame the Pain question, make note of the exact words or phrasing they use to express their pain. Since their words paint images in their minds, when you use their own words in

your conversation they can RELATE to what you are saying because you are conjuring up the images they created!

What's at Stake

Once you know the Lay of the Land and you have identified a need, gently create a sense of urgency around it.
After all, you not only want people to do business with
you, you want them to hire you now rather than later. The
more urgent the problem, the faster people tend to fix it.
If your kitchen sink has a drain that is emptying slowly,
chances are you will put off fixing it for the time being,
even though you know the problem is not going to go
away. But once your drain becomes completely clogged,
you won't waste any time getting the problem fixed. If
there is a problem you can live with, it won't make it to
the top of the proverbial "To Do" list. Chances are you
won't be willing to pay as much for a remedy that isn't
urgent. If on the other hand the pain is severe, action is
often swift and money may become less of an issue. If
your drain is backed up and you can't empty your sink, I
don't think you'll be running around looking for the
cheapest price. You will be looking for someone who can
fix your drain today.

To create a sense of urgency and accelerate the buy
decision, find out "What's at Stake." In other words, find
out what would happen if the problem could be fixed, or
what would happen if the problem were not fixed? For
example, in my consulting practice you may recall, the
two questions I ask are: "What are you currently doing to
open new doors of opportunity?" and then, "What are the
challenges you face in opening those doors?" Now I'm
ready to find out how urgent this problem is. To find out
"What's at Stake" I will ask, "What is the one-time value of
a customer?" If I care to add a greater sense of urgency I

might ask, "What's the lifetime value of a customer?" A one-time value shows what can be gained from acquiring just one additional sale, whereas a lifetime value illustrates an unlimited amount of business that can be gained or lost.

The answer shows both the prospect and me just how important it is to make sure the sales force maximizes every opportunity. It also enables me to point out the return on investment. Since I offer various solutions, this information enables me to know which solution will be the most cost-effective.

You can add a sense of urgency either with a positive bent to your question to stimulate the Greed Glands (what your prospect stands to gain) or with a negative twist to affect the Fear Glands (what your prospect stands to lose). I prefer the positive approach but both work depending on your audience. To give you an example, if you were in the transportation business, your Lay of the Land question could be, "What markets are you currently shipping to?" Your Frame the Pain question could be, "What happens when shipments are late?" To find out What's at Stake you could frame your question in the positive with, "What would it mean to your business if you could rely on shipments to arrive on time?" or frame the question to touch on the Fear Glands with a question like, "What does it cost your business when shipments are late?"

Here's another quick example. If you were a financial consultant targeting individuals saving for retirement, your Lay of the Land question could be "How much are you currently saving for retirement?" Your Frame the Pain question could be, "Do you know how much money you will need to retire?" To find out What's at Stake you could appeal to the Greed Glands with "What do you want to do in retirement?" or play on the Fear Glands by asking "How will you manage if you do not have money to retire on?"

Now that you know how to create your three Control Questions, let's look at how to ask them. If you like you can ask them upfront as a group of questions so your audience has a road map to the conversation. Whenever I introduce these three questions into the conversation all at once I preface the questions by saying, "In order to have a meaningful dialogue I'd like to frame our conversation around these three questions." Then I proceed to mention all three, and then go back to discuss them one at a time.

Another option is to ask your first question, then wait for an answer, then proceed to you second and so on. Since these questions open the conversation to other important qualifying questions, you may actually have several questions in between these three main Control Questions. No matter how you open the conversation, and how many different paths the discussion takes, these three questions will keep your conversation focused. If you ever forget where you are taking the conversation, all you have to remember is which of the three Control Questions you last asked, and then ask the next in sequence.

Enough of me doing all the talking here. It's time to create your own Control Questions. To warm up, let's look at one more example. Suppose you were running an advertising agency. You could get the Lay of the Land by asking something like, "What are you currently doing to market yourself?" The people you are speaking to will no doubt talk about things like brochures, radio, television, Internet, e-commerce, direct marketing, telemarketing, word of mouth, seminars, Yellow Pages, commissioned sales force, resellers and the like. If you see any areas where they have not sought the opportunity to market themselves, you can use this as a point of discussion later. If your prospects say that they use brochures, radio and direct marketing, you would notice a gap because there was no mention of the Internet. You could build a nice business case for that solution. This approach not only opens up opportunities for you, it also leaves a good impression. How so? Well, the way I see it, by pointing out marketing venues they need, you will be adding value to the meeting and adding a layer of credibility to your purpose. After all, any advertising person can sell you media time, but the real value comes in knowing where you need to advertise and how often.

To Frame the Pain, you might ask something like, "What is the objective of those collateral materials?" If the objective was not sales but awareness development, you can use this information to adjust your presentation later by emphasizing the image-building stuff in your portfolio. You can even build on their answer by asking, "How have you managed to generate awareness?" and open the discussion to Frame the Pain even further. To find out What's at Stake and add more urgency, your third Control Question could be, "What does the success of one of those promotions translate into?" You can build on the answer by telling your prospects about your own stats/benchmarks on the success rates of the promotions you create. If someone told you that the success of one promotion is worth a possible five per cent increase in sales, and you just mentioned that your track record shows that you have increased sales for your clients an average of thirty per cent, well I'd say that at this point, your prospect has just made the case for the sale.

I think you're warmed up enough. Get your pen out, clear your thoughts and create your Control Questions. (If you are a born procrastinator, put a bookmark here and come back to this when you have finished reading the book. It's too important to miss.)

Lay of the Land

. . . .
. . . .?

Frame the Pain

. . . .
. . . .?

What's at Stake

. . . .
. . . .?

When people answer these questions, ask yourself if they are addressing your prospect's present needs or future needs. If the Lay of the Land or Frame the Pain reveals that your audience is talking about their situation as it exists today, you need to think about what they might need in the future based on what they have told you. If need be, open the conversation to include their future require- ments. If on the other hand people are telling you about their plans for the future and you know they will need help in certain areas right away, ask them about their pre- sent situation so you both get a more complete picture. For example, if you are selling insurance and I tell you that I'm looking to protect my current income in the event of illness, it doesn't mean that my retirement is planned or that I've given any thought to my estate taxes etc. There is a big picture to consider when you are planning some- one's finances. I might be talking to you about my need for estate planning, but in the meantime, I haven't told you that I currently hold a large mortgage which, as far as you are concerned, means that I need to protect my current income base or else there won't be any estate to concern myself with.

You might want to consider doing a series of Control Questions. Do one generic set that can be used at any time to qualify a customer, and then prepare specific sets of questions which address each of your products. This will help you whenever customers call or drop by to ask about specific products or services. For example, if a customer calls asking you about one of your new graphics software packages, you could instantly take control of the conversation and qualify your customer by asking: "How are you currently creating graphics? What do you use graphics for? What do you want your graphics to deliver that they are not currently providing? If you could create the kind of graphics you just described, what would it mean to your business?"

Here's another example. Suppose you work in a bank and a customer drops by just to renew a short-term investment. It just so happens that you want to do a financial review for your customer, but you can't come right out and ask to do a plan because it will sound like you are selling something. In other words, you'd be going some place your customer does not want to go. Remember, the customer just dropped by for a quick minute to renew a certificate. He or she needs to get back to work. A financial review might be on your agenda, but it is not on your customer's agenda. A review will only happen when your customer agrees to it. Here's where a good Control Question can be of assistance. When the customer says, "I need to renew this certificate. What are your sixty-day rates?" ask what the individual plans on doing with the money.

"Mr. Schwartz, why do you want to cash out? What are you hoping this money is going to do for you? The reason I'm asking is so that I can be sure to recommend an investment that will meet your objectives. For example, you might need your money to be available at a specific date or you might have more flexibility to take advantage of slightly higher rates." After you give Mr. Schwartz rates on some short-term certificates, ask him what his other short-term requirements might be.

"Mr. Schwartz, in order to make sure that you have enough money to meet your other obligations, I'd like to do a brief financial review with your permission. You might have more money put away in short-term investments than you really need, in which case we can reinvest some at higher rates for longer-term requirements, and I also want to check to see if you have any higher-risk investments that might not come through for you when you need short-term cash. Would that be something you would find helpful?" If Mr. Schwartz says "no," he's in a hurry, then at the very least you sounded professional with an offer to provide an important service on his behalf. If Mr. Schwartz agrees that this would be helpful, your customer will WANT TO immediately put your financial review on the agenda.

Each time you use your Control Questions you open up a meaningful dialogue. As the conversation unfolds, you need to maintain your control of the sales call. However, Taking the Reins only gives you control over the direction of the conversation, not over your audience. You never know what people will say or what they are thinking when they are not expressing themselves. To make sure you are connecting with your audience at all times, you have to constantly monitor people's actions, reactions, tone, moods and interest levels. You have to read your audience as carefully as you have been reading this book.

Island 5
Reading the Audience

If there is a single moment when your audience has any unanswered questions, or they do not UNDERSTAND or RELATE to what you are saying at any time, or they are not given an opportunity to contribute to the conversation in a meaningful way, expressing their needs, concerns and viewpoints, they will tune out and disconnect.

Reading the Audience is the glue that holds your sales call together.

I've made Reading the Audience a separate Island of Structure because it is an art and a discipline in its own right. However, unlike the other Islands of Structure that are done at specific points in your sales call, Reading your Audience is done at all times. One of the most valuable lessons I learned from being a professional performer was the ability to read the audience. While a natural gift to many, the ability to read an audience is also a learned skill, which you can master.

How many times have you attended a speech or presentation and noticed how everyone in the room was getting restless and tuning out, and how the person giving the speech never even noticed and kept talking and talking and talking? Do you recall the last time you were in a meeting and didn't UNDERSTAND something someone was presenting, and you felt uncomfortable telling him or her you didn't UNDERSTAND and the person kept talking and talking and talking?

Did you ever figure out why you didn't get that contract signed in the last meeting even though, when you were talking away, you thought everything was going fine?

Such behaviors are all symptomatic of what happens when people don't read their audience. *Every single moment* you are talking with your prospects and customers, you have to make sure that you stay connected with them at all times.

People are either with you or they're not with you. Are you with me?

There are two things you want to watch for: signs that indicate you are connected with your audience, and signs telling you that you have been disconnected (ouch!). If you have been disconnected, you can repair the damage and reconnect if you catch it in time. Let's begin our discussion by having you take your right hand and run it over the top of your head. Let me know if you feel anything unusual. I'll stop writing while you do this . . .

. . . Nothing unusual? I see I have my work cut out for me. OK, put your right hand on the top of your head. Go to the left a little. Down a bit. That's it! Stop right there. What you just discovered is a tiny invisible antenna. It is very real if you tune into it. People are always sending off signals (verbal or physical) as to whether they are tuned in or turned out. That little antenna of yours is designed to pick up those signals. I have prepared a list of signals for you to study which is by no means a definitive one. It is merely a starting point on which to build your own keen observations.

Signs that people are interested:

✓ They are asking questions that move the conversation forward
✓ People elaborate on what you are saying
✓ Show agreement by nodding their heads
✓ Scratching off figures on their pads
✓ Taking notes
✓ Direct eye contact
✓ People lean forward
✓ Animated expressions
✓ Excitement and enthusiasm in their voice
✓ Arms are open
✓ Smiles abound
✓ Constructive suggestions
✓ High energy level
✓ Start to question how your suggestions can be done and what they need to do (a buying signal)
✓ Start to negotiate (another buying signal)
✓ When you lose your train of thought, people remember where you left off
✓ No questions
✓ Silence

Signs that people are tuning out:

✓ They ask questions that move the conversation backward

✓ Side conversations (talking among themselves in an unrelated conversation)

✓ Doodling

✓ People answer the phone

✓ Someone changes the subject

✓ Your audience is not looking at you

✓ People look at their watches

✓ Everyone starts to shuffle papers

✓ Arms are folded across chests

✓ Fidgeting (especially with Type A personalities who are famous for short attention spans)

✓ No note taking

✓ People are not participating

✓ Hands are folded, arms crossed

✓ When you lose your train of thought, no one remembers where you left off

✓ Low energy level

✓ No questions

✓ Silence

I suppose you are really in trouble when people tap their feet, stare at the ceiling, turn their backs to you, start singing, throw heavy objects at your head, or jump out the window. Just kidding. Let's take a serious moment and address two items on the list, namely what happens when there is total silence and what happens when people do not ask questions.

When people are not talking at all, the silence you correctly observe can either be an indication of people tuning in or tuning out. When people are silent, they can just be focused on your every word or thinking intently about an idea you have raised. That happened to me once in a speech where no one said a word or cracked a smile. It turned out that they were a serious group completely focused on my subject matter and soaking it all in. When you notice prolonged silence, observe what happens when you ask a question.

Audience is focused on what you are saying:
• answers questions enthusiastically
• answers in great detail

Audience has tuned out:
• short answers
• incorrect answers
• aren't interested in answering

Take extra care to observe if there is prolonged silence:
• after you make a significant point that requires a lot of thought on the part of the listener
• after you talk about something which is technical
• after you make a controversial statement

These are special moments when your audience has a greater chance of disconnecting. That's because the complexity of your message creates a greater likelihood that people will not UNDERSTAND or RELATE to what you are saying. If you don't get a reaction of any kind after these particular remarks, pay very close attention to the other signs to get a read on whether your audience is tuned in or tuned out. If you find that people have in fact disconnected, go back and communicate your thoughts more clearly, and then ask if there are any questions. Ask people if they agree with your opinion or if they have anything they would like to contribute to the discussion. (This also helps widen the conversation because people with more experience or knowledge will have an opportunity to make a significant contribution to the discussion.)

Continue only after you are satisfied that the meaning behind your message is perfectly clear and understood. Then, after your meeting, make a conscious effort to rephrase your message so people will not disconnect the next time.

Part of the silence you might experience are moments when people are not asking any questions, which can be good and not so good. On the upside, people might not be asking you questions because they might not need to ask; your meaning is crystal clear and they UNDERSTAND and RELATE to everything you are saying. On the downside, some people might not be asking questions because they are uncomfortable doing so, especially when there are many people in the meeting. It is important to know how to deal with a situation where people are not asking questions because communication is a two-way street and you run the risk of a one-way conversation if you do not engage your audience.

If you ever find yourself in a sales call where you are not being asked any questions, you'll know soon enough whether your upside or downside is showing simply by stopping what you are doing and asking if there are any questions. If you still do not get any questions, proceed for a few minutes and then ask someone to recap what he or she has heard or learned so far. "Steven, how do you feel about what we've been discussing?" or, "Which point is most important to you?" Another way to know what's behind the silence is to simply observe if the other signals your trusty antenna has picked up (the signals we just listed a moment ago) are telling you that people are tuned in or tuned out.

While it is important to know how to deal with a situation where people are not asking questions, it is equally important to UNDERSTAND how to be prepared when people do ask questions. Even though your audience is tuned in, you need checkpoints along the way to help reveal if people are on board with your point of view: do they agree with your position? Are they sitting on the fence? Have they dismissed you altogether? As my good friend Don Carr says: *just as you have to be ready, willing and able to do business with your prospects, they too must reach the same state of mind to agree to proceed.*

So when you are reading the audience and you see that they are tuned in and listening, how do you know if they are really *ready* to commit? They won't be if their questions are unanswered or they have not been given ample time to have their thoughts heard. Even though you have people's attention, they might not be *willing* to have a relationship with you because they have not bought into your idea or your terms, even though they have articulated a need. By the same token, you can have people's attention but they are not *able* to commit because they do not have the signing authority to make this deal happen.

The questions people ask and the dialogue they open up shed light on all these prerequisites for success, and more. The art of handling questions is just so important that we're going to devote extra time to the subject.

Handling Questions

Think about the last time you sat down with a salesperson when you were looking to make a purchase. What did you think of the salesperson when they didn't have an answer to one of your questions? What did you think when the person gave you an answer you were not satisfied with, or worse, just brushed it off altogether? Did it leave you with confidence in the individual? Did you trust that person? Were you not frustrated for some time, perhaps even for the remainder of the meeting? Now consider the flip side: how did you react when the salesperson gave you a really passionate response without hesitation? I would venture that you figured that this person knew their stuff, and you probably could sense their confidence.

Many people are uncomfortable with fielding questions. Personally, I'm more uncomfortable if people are not asking any questions. Questions are wonderful. They are a form of audience participation that generates energy, fuels passion and creates an environment of learning. Most important, your ability to effectively answer questions builds trust, and trust is the foundation of any relationship. Answers that are meaningful make you sound professional and give you credibility; they send the message that you know your subject matter and you have experience discussing this matter with other people. Effective answers create clarity. *Clarity is the foundation of persuasion.* Only when your meaning is clear can you move the conversation forward. Clarity also means that people can better UNDERSTAND and RELATE to your message, and therefore on the basis of what you have to say. For all these reasons, effective answers have the power to shorten your sales cycle.

Being prepared with effective answers prevents you from getting sidetracked and blown off course. It keeps you in control. As well, a knock-out answer to a tough question can, at times, mean the difference between a deal breaker and a deal maker. Have you ever watched a televised political debate and seen a politician's career come to an abrupt end when he had no comeback to a direct question? It was over in seconds. On the flip-side, there have been many political figures who won an election simply because they had an effective response that wowed the voters and caught their opponents off-guard.

One of the reasons why people are skittish about taking questions is the concern that they might run out of time. If you have lots of time in your sales call or presentation, you can invite people to ask questions at any time. If you are pressed for time, you can control the situation by requesting that people hold their questions until the end. This way you get to finish your presentation on time. You'll then be able to manage questions more effectively later on without feeling pressured. I do this quite often when I give speeches and seminars.

Another concern people have about taking questions is what to do if they don't have an answer to any particular question. There is a simple remedy. Simply be prepared with a response like, "That's an excellent question. I'll get back to you on that by 3:00 today." Make sure you do. Tons of deals are lost every day when salespeople do not follow through. Just last week I went to purchase a pair of glasses. I wasn't sure how the lenses for my prescription would look on the frameless style, so the optician said that she would check with the lens manufacturer and call me the next day to let me know. Two days passed. No call. So I took my purchasing power elsewhere and another optician got the sale instead. Keeping a commitment speaks to your professionalism and credibility. It builds trust and establishes more solid relationships. It's also just plain good business.

Some people also worry about losing control of the conversation or losing credibility with their audience if the questions they offer are not accepted. Preparation is once again your best friend. You can keep control of your meeting and impress your audience with your professionalism by anticipating the most-asked questions and then preparing effective answers. Of course, all of this assumes that you know your product and service offerings inside out. If you don't know what you are selling, how can you be confident about answering questions? You can't.

Having effective answers to your most-asked questions is not something you can leave to chance. (Chance means you are not in control.) Creating answers to your most-asked questions is something you prepare in advance and build over time. (Preparation puts you in control.) I call it a Question Portfolio, much like the Objections Portfolio you may have already applied from *How To Make Hot Cold Calls*. Here's how you put it together:

After each meeting, keep track of the questions that you were asked and the responses you gave. If they were effective, remember them so you can use them again. If your answers were less than satisfactory, redo them and test them again over the course of the next meeting or two. Continue this simple process until you have effective answers that you have complete confidence in.

In your Question Portfolio, make a point of listing the subject matter. This will make it easier for you to locate the questions for any individual sales call, and will also show you the areas where you need to brush up on your product or service knowledge.

QUESTION PORTFOLIO

Subject: . . . .

Question: . . . .

. . . .

Response:

. . . .

. . . .

Each time you enhance your Question Portfolio, reward yourself. A basic law of human nature is, activity that gets rewarded gets done.

As you create your portfolio of responses, keep in mind that an effective answer is one that is written from the customer's perspective. It is focused on what is important to them, not you. If you asked me, "Steven, how long does it take to train a salesperson to make successful sales calls?" I could answer it from my perspective, "Six weeks." But if I know that the reason why someone is asking the question is because they are concerned about taking their salespeople away from their customers for any length of time, I would answer, "It takes six weeks while they go about their daily business." Over time your experience will teach you why people ask you certain questions, and you can use that knowledge to build answers that will be more meaningful to your audience.

If in the meantime you are not sure why someone is asking a question, simply ask them to clarify their concerns. A big part of understanding what someone is really asking you is knowing why they are asking. So suppose you were to ask me, "Steven, do presentations require a lot of preparation?" I might check on why you are asking the question so that I know what kind of answer to give. I'd probably ask you, "Are you asking that question to find out what kind of preparation is involved, or do you have a concern over tight time constraints?" If you tell me you have to know what's involved, my answer will include all the details about the preparation. If you were asking because you did not think that you would have enough time, I would make sure my answer includes information on how long each part of the preparation takes and how to save time. I'd probably even remind you that since your objective is to make effective presentations, there is no substitute for preparation, and the time you invest will show in the results you get. You don't need to restate every question. Just do so when you are asked questions that can have several different answers and you need to know which answer to provide.

As you test the effectiveness of your responses on your audience, you will know if you're hitting home runs because your audience will nod their approval or tell you that they now UNDERSTAND your thoughts better. Otherwise, ask your audience directly. For example, after I answer a question I often verify that people understood by asking something like, "Did that answer your question?" or, "Was that the information you were looking for?" or, "Was that answer helpful?" This not only ensures that I eventually give them an answer they are satisfied with, but also shows my audience that I respect them and that I value their contribution, all of which goes toward building an even stronger relationship. Of course, someone could just be polite and say "yes," so I always stay vigilant in adjusting my antenna (yes I have one too) to pick up any signs that my audience may be tuning out.

Should people tell you that they are not happy with your answer, don't take it personally and don't be surprised. You are simply being presented with yet another great learning opportunity. First, it is a signal indicating that you need to find out why they are asking the question so that you better UNDERSTAND what the customers is really concerned about. It can also help you gain insight into the type of people you are dealing with. For example, someone might ask you to go into more detail, perhaps because the individual is the analytical type who craves details. (When this is the case, make sure to add more details throughout your presentation.) When your audience tells you what kind of answer they are looking for,

they are showing you what a complete answer to that
question should look like. Once you know this, you will be
better prepared to answer it correctly the next time.
Perhaps most important, customers' questions will give
you greater insight into how they view things and what is
really important to them.

What's important to your audience is important to you.

When you are confident that you are clear about what
their concerns are, answer the question as best you can. If
people do not agree with your answer or point of view,
open it up for discussion. Ask them why they do not
agree. You want to make sure that everyone genuinely disagrees with your answer rather than simply disagreeing
with what *they thought you said*. Get people to clarify
their thoughts and find out what the real issues or concerns are. For example, if you were discussing the delivery
of an item, your audience might be fine with the price but
not comfortable with the time it takes to deliver the goods
or the way the goods are being shipped. Once you know
where the roadblock is, you can take steps to remove it. In
the example I just gave, you could either offer other shipping arrangements or explain why your shipping is done
a certain way. Always be sure to explain your position, or
else you run the risk that your audience will tune out and
disconnect. If, for instance, someone who disagrees with
you is clearer in explaining his or her position than you
are, other people in the room might go with their colleague's position—and you will lose your audience.

It's worth noting that as a professional, people expect
you to have an opinion. When you express a professional
opinion and have the experience, conviction and passion
to back it up, people are often impressed because you

obviously believe in what you are saying. Never get defensive. If someone feels equally passionate about a point of view, just respect where he or she is coming from and agree to disagree. If you are proven wrong on an issue, it's always nice to thank the person for sharing the insight. We can all learn something from everyone. When someone does not agree with one of my methods I invite that person to test the new approach along with mine. Whichever approach works best is the one they should continue with. "After all," I explain, "your success is the objective here." If the approach works best I like to hear about it so I can share the experience with others.

If you express a professional opinion that is controversial in any way, you will need to take extra care to make sure your audience is on board. For example, in my corporate training I'm a big believer in one-on-one coaching, which is central to the structure of my learning methodology. I need to test the waters to see if my prospect also believes in the value of coaching or else I will lose that person. To verify that the person is with me on this issue, I often state my belief that most training fails because of a lack of follow-through. People are often trained in the classroom and then given no support or resources once they are out in the world where they need to apply what they have learned. After stating my opinion I always ask: "Have you found that to be the case?" or, "Has that been your experience?" In this way I give people an opportunity to express their opinion; if they disagree I can strengthen my case by citing examples, and if they agree they have already sold themselves on my learning methodology.

With all this talk about how to create effective answers, there is a flip side equally important to note.

Why wait to be asked a question in the first place?

Any question that goes unanswered causes frustration until it is answered. If people are sitting there not knowing what you are talking about (and who knows for how long they've been sitting there lost), the frustration creates tons of damaging negative energy that silently kills deals.

Unanswered questions put you at risk of disconnecting.

When people do not UNDERSTAND something, they will tune out and you'll never know what hit you when you don't get the sale. That's assuming of course that people will actually get around to asking the question in the first place. Thinking that someone who has a question will ask that question is a very big assumption and a hidden danger to avoid. Just because people are not asking a question, doesn't mean they don't have one that's gnawing away unanswered in their minds.

Let's look at some preventive medicine:

After your meeting when you are self-assessing the effectiveness of your answers, review why someone felt compelled to ask a question in the first place. If that person needed clarification on an earlier point you made, make sure you communicate that point more clearly the next time. If you don't do this, you might not be asked the same question again, and things will remain fuzzy and ineffective.

Up to this point, everything we've talked about in handling questions is designed to create an environment that encourages people to speak up while at the same time reducing the need for them to ask you in the first place. What you've seen is that questions are useful to both parties. Your audience gets clarity and you get an opportunity to read your audience, stay connected and move the sales cycle forward by building trust. My mother was right when she taught me that there is no such thing as a silly question.

The cool thing about questions is that they are constantly showing you the direction in which your conversation is headed. Those signals beam straight into your antenna, which is why you need to listen very, very carefully to the questions being asked to know whether you are connected with your audience. There are basically two types of questions you need to tune into, and in fact, you already came across them in the sections "Signs that people are interested" and "Signs that people are tuning out." Do you remember what they were? (They are the very first points on each list.)

The two types of questions are those that move the conversation forward and those that move it backward. It reminds me of a scene in the classic movie *The Wizard of Oz* when the Good Witch of the North comes down and asks the newly arrived Dorothy, "Are you a good witch or a bad witch?" I'm always playing this in my mind when questions come up. "Are you a good question or a bad question?" Good questions move you forward and bad questions move you backward.

When you keep the conversation moving forward you are headed to a positive conclusion because it's a sign people are tuned in and turned on. You are connected. When you slip backward it's a warning sign that people are tuning out and turning off, perhaps because there is something they don't UNDERSTAND or RELATE to, or there is something they don't agree with and they haven't expressed their difference of opinion. If you ignore this signal long enough, you will lose your audience and your sale altogether. As soon as you sense that you are going backward, the alarm bells from your antenna should go off and get you to take corrective action so you can get your conversation moving forward. Immediately.

Some of the questions that move the conversation forward include:

Questions focused on the future. When people are inquiring about possibilities, it is a sign that you are moving forward. "Steven, where do we go from here?" "How many people do you need to work with?" "What sort of timing are we looking at?" You are most likely reading a buying signal.

Detailed "If" questions. "Steven, if we can arrange a tour of our facilities, can you find the information you are looking for?"

Analytical questions. These indicate that people are taking what you are saying seriously as they study all the possibilities and implications of what you are proposing. "How do you go about achieving that?" "Explain to me how that works."

Questions that build on your last point. When people add to your discussion this way, they have listened to what you've said and have understood your message. They are going the extra step by participating in the discussion and they are adding value by taking your thoughts to the next level. When this happens the energy in the room increases and more thoughts are generated as a result. The good news is that they are building on your last point, not tearing it down. You have support from a member of your audience, which can persuade others in your audience to support your position as well.

"Can you elaborate on that?" These words are music to my ears. This is a signal that people are clearly interested in what you are saying and they WANT TO know

more. Sometimes people might ask you to elaborate for
clarification, but the fact that they asked the question
should tell you that they are interested in what you
have to say and want to UNDERSTAND you completely. When people make the effort to UNDERSTAND your
message, you are more likely to stay connected.

**Any question on price once the value proposi-
tion is understood.**
For example, if clients see value in what you are offering and they are asking about price, they are exploring
options and looking for ways to fit it into their budget.
That is not to say that they will not try to negotiate the
price, but they are already moving the conversation
forward by looking at how they can make the purchase
happen.

Some of the questions that move the conversation backward include:
**Any question on price when there is no per-
ceived value.** Anything is expensive when the value is
not understood. That goes for a one-dollar purchase
just as much as for a forty-thousand-dollar purchase. If
people ask why something is expensive, your antenna
should alert you to the fact that somewhere in your
conversation you had a disconnect from your audience; they did not UNDERSTAND the real value behind
what they are paying for.
Questions that are off topic. It's like driving north
with someone who all of a sudden decides to take the
wheel and head east. When this happens you might
never get back on course and arrive at your intended
destination.
"Can you go over this again?" When people seek
clarification on a point, it is a sign that they clearly do

not UNDERSTAND or RELATE to some or your entire message. You need to find out *exactly* what they don't UNDERSTAND and then self-assess after the sales call to find out how you lost them. Then take corrective measures to make sure that your meaning is clearer the next time around.

"I'm not comfortable with that." If individuals do not agree with something you have said or they don't care for something you are suggesting, your conversation and your sales call may very well come to a full stop. As I mentioned earlier, you need to stop in your tracks and find out why they are not on board.

"Can you repeat that question?" Either people did not hear you the first time or they heard you but did not UNDERSTAND what you were asking. You need to make sure that you are not talking quickly or using terms and buzz words your audience cannot RELATE to. Sometimes it is not the question they did not UNDERSTAND but rather that the information leading up to the question got lost somehow.

Someone keeps coming back to the same question. When this happens, it could either be because your answer is not clear or your audience cannot RELATE to your response. It might also be an indication that someone has a serious concern about something and, hence, keeps coming back to it. If this is the case you have just been given a clear signal on how important this issue is to this person. It will have to be fully addressed in order to move the sales cycle forward. When people come back to the same question, listen closely to hear if they ask it in the same words. Sometimes people rephrase a question because they are looking for a better answer, one that is either clearer or more in line with their point of view or agenda.

In any event, make sure people clarify their thoughts to find out why they are asking the question.

Whether questions move your conversation forward or backward, they give you insight into the type of people you are dealing with. For example, many Type A personalities want you to get to the point quickly because they are focused on making decisions and getting results. This group tends to ask direct close-ended questions, like the kind beginning with "What…" or "When…" For example, rather than ask an open-ended question like, "How long do you suggest we need to roll out this program?" they would more likely ask "What is your time line for rolling this out?" or, "Are you suggesting we roll this out in two weeks?" Those kinds of questions are designed to get short or single-word answers. So when you read that your audience is Type A, give them the kind of answers they are looking for: short and to the point. If during a presentation you notice people fidgeting and you already know that they are Type A personalities, this behavior will be your cue to either pick up the pace, make your answers shorter, get to your main points faster, and/or make your conversation more meaningful and relevant to their situation.

Your analytical types will be just the opposite. They will take their time making decisions because they like to carefully review all the facts. This group tends to ask open-ended questions, like the kind beginning with "Why…" and "How…." They want you to give them the facts slowly so that they have time to digest and analyze every single detail. They can never get enough details. Take your time answering there questions and pour on the facts and figures.

You will inevitably come across people who are big on relationships and think in terms of the team. "How do we do this together?" They need to know how they will reach a decision that includes everyone's input and agreement. In fact, if people are not allowed to express their thoughts, this type of person is not comfortable proceeding. So when you answer a question, include everyone in the discussion by asking others how they feel about the answer or if there is anything they would like to add.

All in all, the more you know about your audience— from the types of people they are to the questions they ask and the gestures they make— the easier it will be to keep your conversation moving forward. Just keep your antenna tuned into all the various signals you have just learned and don't worry if you miss a few when you start. Look for a few signs in each sales call and then add in new signs at each subsequent meeting. Anticipate that at first you might miss a few signs or misread them, or you might come across objections and questions you have not known about. Do your best at that moment and then learn from the experience. I'm a big believer in that.

Every sales call is a valuable resource to learn from.

At the end of the sales call, self-assess what you did well so you can repeat it later. Also review where you went wrong so you will not make the same mistakes the next time around. Remember the signs you overlooked and make note of how you need to better handle them in the future. Build on your Question Portfolio. Then reward yourself for learning from your mistakes. By doing this, you will master the art of reading your audience in no time at all.

Now in the event that you misread a signal at the beginning of your learning curve, there are steps you can take to reconnect with your audience regardless of what type of personalities you are dealing with. If you do lose your audience, no problem. Don't be shy. Stop and ask if there are any questions. Clarity is everything. Questions are a great way to test if your audience is listening. You can also get people to reflect back on what you are saying, something like, "Steven, how do you feel about that?" or, "Steven, what has your experience been in this area?" You can also try to get them to do something, like participating in a demonstration of some kind. This can often restart conversations and thought processes and elevate the energy in the room.

Energy is an important barometer to monitor. If you are presenting to an audience at the end of the day, chances are they might very well be tired. If you are a high-energy person you have to be careful not to overpower people with an energetic delivery until they have had a chance to warm up or wake up. If you sense that the audience is tired, hold back a bit on your passion or any jokes you might want to tell. The last thing you want happening is to say something humorous and not get any response. When I'm giving speeches I often include a joke within the first five minutes to test the water. If the response is great, I'll pour on the energy. If not, I'll hold back on the other bits of humor and pull back on my passionate delivery until my audience is ready for it. To energize your audience, all you have to do is get them involved right away. Ask a question. Get them thinking about something. As the energy in the room begins to increase you will see people leaning forward and watching you more intently, taking notes, asking questions and generally participating more. If half way into your sales call or presentation you notice the energy decreasing, this may be a sign that you are losing your audience. If that happens, take the corrective measures you have now learned and reconnect with your audience. It's all within your control.

I was taking a cab to the airport on the return home from a recent trip to Chicago. The delightful driver, Anthony Mack, told me with great pride how he makes a point of always reading his audience. It turns out that Anthony tests the water by engaging his passengers in a little small talk, and if they reciprocate he continues to carry on the conversation. However, if he senses that his audience is not in a talkative mood, he immediately keeps quiet until his passengers have arrived safely at their destination. Anthony's ability to read the mood of his audience keeps his customers happy, and his wallet filled with generous tips.

Island 6
Verifying

Look how far you've come. There you are on a sales call and you made a great first impression. You made sure to turn your audience on and tune them in, you have taken the reins to get a good sense of what your prospect needs, and you stayed connected by reading your audience at every glance. Since you have the attention of your audience and you have already determined how you can help them, there is just one more thing to do before you tell them how you can be of service.

Verify that what your audience said was in fact what you heard. How many times have people told you something and then you find out that what you thought they said was not actually what they meant, or what was said? Before you go off talking about your offerings for the remainder of the discussion, make sure that the road you are on is one your audience will WANT TO travel down.

Verify their story before you tell your story.

After you Take the Reins (Lay of the Land, Frame the

Pain, What's at Stake) review what your audience has told you. Something like, "Allow me to recap what I've learned so far." Or "Let me see if I've heard you correctly." Here's an example, "Allow me to recap what I've learned so far. Your company is opening a new store in September and your biggest concern is coordinating your suppliers with your main warehouse so that you can keep up with the anticipated rush in new orders. Otherwise you will lose market share. Is that correct?"

At this point your prospects can confirm that you got it right, correct you, change their minds or add something they forgot to mention. If people have something new to add at this point, your conversation can easily move in a very different direction. They might have told you twenty minutes ago that their biggest concern is coordinating their suppliers with their main warehouse, but since you have recapped the conversation, the VP has had a change of thought and decided that the biggest issue isn't inventory; it's the delivery people who are late with the orders. Now you are going to have all the correct information you need to qualify the opportunity.

The need to make sure that all the information is on the table is doubly important when you are addressing more than one person in a sales call. Sometimes because of group dynamics some people do not open up and contribute to the conversation. They might have been analytical types who were quietly observing everything, or they might not have been comfortable speaking in a group situation, or perhaps some senior people were monopolizing the conversation. In any event, you need to give these people the opportunity to express their points of view.

Suppose you are a financial consultant and you are meeting with two business partners who are clients of yours. One of them tells you that they have $30,000 to invest (Lay of the Land), and that they need to invest the money only for the short term to cover possible cash flow requirements (Frame the Pain), and they can't have anything risky because the government won't wait for their tax installments (What's at Stake). When you verify what you heard, the other partner, who hadn't said much up until this point, explains, "Well actually we only need $10,000 for tax installments and $10,000 for cash flow. The rest can be invested a little more aggressively." This new information clarifies their needs and will open up new investment opportunities for you to recommend. Don't you feel good about having asked the question?

I remember a meeting where a VP told me that his biggest issue was training new people, and yet when I verified what he said, another VP in the same meeting noted that the main issue was not training at all but product knowledge, and yet a third person disagreed with her colleagues and said that the issue was the ability of the sales managers to reach decision makers. It was a good thing that I verified because otherwise I would have proceeded without two of the three prospects on board, and the likelihood of securing a contract would have been slim at best. As it turned out, I let them have a healthy discussion before reaching a consensus. In the meantime, my audience stayed connected and I was able to then offer the appropriate solution.

Now that your customer's needs have been articulated and agreed to, you are ready to talk about how you can be of help to meet their needs. When you talk about a solution at this stage it will seem completely natural. You won't be perceived as someone just trying to sell something. Your audience will WANT TO hear what you have to offer because at this point it is in their best interest to do so.

Island 7
The Solution

When you are ready to talk about your products, begin by immediately establishing a connection between your offering and their needs. You can do this by reiterating the exact words that your audience used to describe their needs when you Framed the Pain and found out What's at Stake. There are two reasons why you use *their* words. The first is to send a signal that you have been listening. When people know you have been listening to them, they are more motivated to listen to you. The second reason to put their own words back into the conversation is because people RELATE to their own words and the images these words create (they are, after all, their words). Your audience is also describing concerns and needs that are very real to them. You solicit your prospect's undivided attention by talking about what's important to them. (You are activating the Greed Glands, remember?)

The words we speak paint images in our mind, and we move in the images we create.

So when our own words come back to us, we are drawn to them on an emotional level because the images they portray are very real to us. Allow me to give you a very basic example of the process in action. Let's suppose you are a financial consultant and you were talking to me for the first time in a face-to-face sales call. Watch how the conversation unfolds as you discover the Lay of the Land, Frame the Pain and find out What's at Stake, and then use my words when you offer a solution.

You: Steven, how are you currently managing your money?

Me: I have short-term, mid-term and long-term investments.

You: Are you diversified?

Me: I think so. I keep my money with several banks.

You: Diversified really has more to do with having your investments in different parts of the market.

Me: That would be true for all my investments.

You: Do you have a financial plan for short-term, mid-term and long-term objectives?

Me: No, but I regularly buy a lot of bonds for short-term cash for a little added security.

You: Is security important to you?

Me: I'm not adverse to risk if it's long term, but anything short-term has to be fairly risk-free.

You: What are you most concerned about?

Me: I need to always keep a certain amount of money on hand to meet immediate or unexpected financial obligations. You know, cash flow.

You: What are the challenges you are facing with building up your cash flow?

Me: Keeping the tax man off my back.

You: Which means…

Me: Tax installments.

You: What's at stake if you don't have enough to cover your taxes?

Me: Need to cash in other investments, and I stand to lose money if I'm pulling out of a good investment just to cash it in for tax installments. If I'm cashing in bonds I can lose money if it's locked in at a high rate and then the rates go down after I cash them out.

You: Let me review what I've learned so far. Your money is diversified in short- to long- term investments, there is no formal plan in place and your main concern is making your tax installments. Is that correct?

Me: You got it.

You: Well, in order to keep the tax man off your back and secure your cash flow, I have an interesting solution I think you will find most helpful. May I share it with you?

Notice that at no time was there any mention of product or service offerings until the needs were articulated by the customer and verified by the financial adviser. Just for fun, let's stop for a minute and look at how I might have reacted if you were talking about your products too early.

You: Steven, how are you currently managing your money?

Me: I have short-term, mid-term and long-term investments.

You: Are you diversified?

Me: I think so. I keep my money with several banks.

You: Diversified really has more to do with having your

investments in different parts of the market. We have several financial products I can show you that can help you diversify your investments. (Rambles on about various products.)

Stop the Press! Doesn't it sound like you are about to push the financial product of the month on me? You don't even know my main beef, which is cash flow for tax installments. I might not be diversified, and all right maybe I need to be, but it's not on the top of my "to do" list. You didn't even ask me if diversifying was important to me, let alone ask what else might be valuable.

Such is the danger you run into when mentioning your product or service offerings before a need is articulated and agreed to. Your prospect is now no longer.

When you look at the first example, did you notice the impact of the last question, where you asked, "May I share it with you?" This little phrase packs a lot of power because it allows you to subtly read the audience to make sure you are connected. Here's what I mean. When you ask, "May I share it with you?" someone is either going to say "Yes" or "No." Correct? Let's walk through the scenarios. Keep in mind that your audience may either verbalize their permission by saying something like "Yes, go on" or they might just use their body language by nodding. If they indicate nothing at all, assume it's all right to proceed.

YES scenario: people WANT TO know
NO scenario: unasked/unanswered questions

If people give you permission to proceed they are in a WANT TO frame of mind, which is precisely where you want them. You have their undivided attention. You will also notice that their energy level picks up because they are excited about what you are about to tell them. You can feed off that energy as it gives you even more confidence to proceed. And what if they say "NO?" That can happen and if it ever does you'll be glad you asked the question in the first place.

The reason individuals may not give you permission to proceed is because they might have a question or two that has been lingering. They may have asked a question and not been satisfied with your answer, or they may have simply not asked the question at all. What was the question? I'm glad you asked…

You: Well, in order to keep the tax man off your back and secure your cash flow, I have an interesting solution I think you'll be interested in. May I share it with you?

Me: Before you tell me, I still have a question about what you meant about a financial plan.

It's a good thing you asked "May I share it with you?" What if you had just jumped in to talk about your solution and I was sitting there frustrated because of this lingering question in my mind. You would experience disconnection from your audience. What if this question was to go on lingering for some time? It would only build and build and all the while everything you would be discussing would be going in one ear and out the other. There would also be a risk that I would not UNDERSTAND and RELATE to what you'd be talking about, in which case I would not take action and worse, you would have no idea at the end of the sales call why I would not be interested in proceeding to the next step.

As well as preventing disconnection from your audience, this technique also does a wonderful job at recon-

necting you in the event you disconnected earlier and did-
n't catch it. People might bring up questions that they
were sitting on twenty minutes ago and now you can
reconnect by addressing their issues at this most oppor-
tune time.

I have a really interesting story I'd love to share with
you right now. May I? (Was that a YES I heard?) One of my
clients named Francois was in a sales call with an existing
customer and just as he was about to present a solution to
a need that was articulated and verified, Francois asked
the prospect, "May I share it with you?" Guess what happened? Right then his customer asked Francois, "Could
you wait a few minutes while I deal with something in the
other room?" to which Francois replied "Certainly." The
customer went off to talk with someone in the hall. It
turns out that a colleague was waving his arms trying to
get this fellow's attention at the office window to tell him
that he was needed in another meeting for a few minutes.
When the customer returned, he was all-ears, giving
Francois his undivided attention. The point of this true
story has never been lost on Francois. Had he not asked
permission to present the solution and proceeded to talk
about it, he would have only had half of the customer's
attention, if that, since this fellow's mind was clearly elsewhere which would have dramatically reduced the likelihood of a successful conclusion. As it turned out, Francois
was able to stay connected with his customer, have a
meaningful conversation and close a lucrative deal.

Whatever the solution you happen to be sharing, make
sure it is not just what clients want, but what they need. I
know there are many schools of thought on this. Some
profess that if people want something, give it to them. It's
their business whether they need it. But there is another
school of thought that I subscribe to which says that in

order to build trust, you recommend a solution that is truly needed. This is not as easy as it sounds because sometimes people know what they want but don't know what they need. If you were selling pets and I came to you because I wanted a golden retriever, you know what I want but is it really what I need? If you qualified my need by asking if I had anyone in the house with allergies and I told you yes, you would recommend a dog that doesn't shed. I would then either take your advice and thank you for pointing that out and saving me a lot of problems down the road, or I would still insist on buying a retriever from you, but I would respect your honesty and know you are someone I can trust.

If you find yourself in a situation where your customers have a few needs and there are several products or services that you can offer, or they have one need with numerous solutions that would apply, address one need or solution at a time. You don't want to run the risk of overwhelming customers with too many choices and decisions.

By the way, if it turns out that someone needs something that you don't offer, walk away from the business or refer them to someone who can be of service. Don't try to offer me a size ten shoe when what I really need is a nine-and-a-half. That's not the way to win repeat business or generate referrals.

Right now your customer is far from walking away. The customer has told you what is needed, you have listened diligently and responded with an appropriate solution. There will likely be lots of discussion around your solution, and once all questions have been answered to the satisfaction of your audience, you will have arrived at the moment of truth where the sale needs to be concluded.

Island 8
The Close

"I gotta close this deal."

"What do I do now? How do I ask them to sign up?"

"My bonus is riding on this one."

"If I don't close this sale I'm not going to make my numbers."

"C'mon. C'mon. Make up your mind already. Hurry up and just buy!"

A little anxious are we? Relax, you have company. There are millions of people who are stressed out over closing a sale. To make matters worse, most managers are breathing down everyone's neck waiting for the contracts to come in, and right behind them are the shareholders waiting for the quarterly numbers. Of course, if you run a small enterprise you are sensitive to the fact that if you don't close you can't pay your staff and what kind of business are you going to have then? If you are self-employed you have to pay your bills and keep that line of credit from running dry.

The more you need the sale, the more anxious you become. The more anxious you become, the more likely the sale doesn't happen because you come across as being too anxious for it. Ever walk into a store and the salespeople are on you before you even take five steps? You can tell who is on commission and who isn't. (In fact, the higher your commission structure, the more anxious you become. The self-employed fall into this category too.)

There is a popular upscale men's clothing store in Toronto where you are followed around the floor by commissioned salespeople; it actually feels more like being shadowed. The first time this happened to me I wanted to turn around and shout "Boo!" to the shadow.

Anxious doesn't cut it.

The pressure to make a sale is real, and the angst around closing is as old as the marketplace. Closing has become not just a focal point in sales, but *the* focal point. I'm not suggesting for a moment that closing is not important. I'm just making the point that closing is not as big a deal as it's made out to be.

If I was trying to sell something that a person didn't want or need, then I'd have every reason to be anxious about closing because the person might wise up and figure out he's being manipulated. But if I'm offering a good solution to a problem someone has expressed, I don't need to worry.

Closing is not the single moment of truth. It's the culmination of a lot of preparation on your part. No one can win the gold medal all the time. You can't win every sale but you can do everything possible to create an environment where your customers WANT TO buy from you. At the very least you can have a positive engagement where you earn the respect of your audience, and by doing so you leave the door open for future business when the timing is better.

Closing reminds me of an exam at school. Do you remember the times when you were up the night before a final exam worried sick about how well you would perform, especially with so much riding on the results? But do you also remember how you felt those times when you actually took the time to study for your exam and you knew your subject inside out? Didn't you have a restful sleep? If you do your homework as we've outlined so far, your closing should look after itself.

If you want a repeat customer and long-term relationship, closing should not under any circumstances be forced. If you and your prospect have clearly identified and articulated a need (Taking the Reins) that you and your prospect clearly UNDERSTAND (Verifying), if you can articulate a solution to what the customer wants and activate the Greed Glands (The Solution), and your audience does in fact UNDERSTAND and RELATE to what you are saying (Reading the Audience), then you have done all you possibly can to create an environment to close so that people will take action!

Closing should be as gentle as a feather when you create the environment to close.

Once you have discussed your solution you may decide to give a brief presentation on your product or solution, which you will have prepared in advance (which you will learn how to do in the second part of this book). Your discussion around your solution will no doubt open up the conversation and chances are your customer will have some questions and even some objections, and you'll have to be prepared with effective responses as we discussed earlier. After you have verified that all the questions have been answered satisfactorily, it is quite natural to close on the commitment to go forward with the next phase of the sales cycle.

Closing is simply asking for permission to go the next step, whatever that step happens to be.

Actually, the ultimate scenario is that your customers close you first. In my nearly quarter-century of self-employment, I can't recall a single instance where I asked for a contract. My customers closed me with remarks like "Sounds good Steven, where do we go from here?" or, "What do you need from us to get started?" The reason why people will close you is because it is evidently clear to them that you have something they need, right away, at a price they are willing to pay.

But that's not the only reason why people will give you permission to go to the next step. After all, unless you have a monopoly, they can still take their business elsewhere. I'd venture to say that the other reason is the rapport you built with your audience; you created a good first impression, engaged your audience and opened up a conversation; you stayed connected with people, earned the right to advance and move the conversation forward by listening to their needs instead of trying to push a product on them, and only after identifying a need and verifying their story did you respectfully ask if you could discuss a solution that meets their requirements; you even managed to earn their trust by passionately answering all their questions. In short, you simply created an environment where people WANT TO do business with you.

Even before people close you, they are sending signals

that tell you when they have moved from interest to action. Some of them you may already know.

What are the common buying signals you have observed from past experience?

. . . .

. . . .

Your experience is something to learn from and build on. After each sales call, self-assess and make note of each new buying signal you observed so you can program your antenna to tune into that frequency the next time. For example, recall and jot down from past experience buying signals you observed at moments when:

- Customers start to negotiate
- They ask "If" questions, such as "If I get this to you by Monday can you get me the quote by Thursday?"
- Your audience starts internal discussions on what this sale might mean
- They ask you, "Where do we go from here? What do we need to do to make this happen?"
- Or, they start to talk about possible obstacles that might get in the way

Whatever the buying signals, keep your antenna tuned. When you see them, it's time for the close. One of the biggest mistakes salespeople make is selling past the close. If you are presenting a series of overheads and someone stops you and says "How soon can you start?" don't say, "Just a moment, I have another six slides to show you." (I actually witnessed just such a moment once.) Recognize that the person is ready to commit to the next step. Immediately move the conversation in that direction.

If you pick up buying signals and your prospective customer is not closing you, it's up to you to take control. I see nothing wrong with being assumptive, especially since you have uncovered the needs, qualified the opportunity and your audience agrees that your solution is a good fit. So for example, if you were discussing the painting of my house you could simply ask, "Can we go over the details of setting up the paint job?" or, "Will you be home next week so I can have your house finished before your party?" If you've been talking with someone about office supplies you could simply close by asking, "Are you planning to have these supplies delivered or will you make the pick-up yourself?" If you were an insurance agent discussing disability insurance with someone, you might close with, "Mr. Reebuck, when would you be available for the medical examination?" If you created the right environment to close and Mr. Reebuck has no more questions and no objection to a medical, he will more than likely tell you when he is free and will agree to a medical.

Make it easy for the customer to buy.

Make sure you have made it easy for people to take that next step. If you need Mr. Reebuck to take an examination, give him options of possible dates so you don't have to call him back. If there are any procedures Mr. Reebuck needs to follow for the examination, give him a checklist on a reminder sheet that you can walk him through and answer any questions right then and there. Remember, don't assume that Mr. Reebuck will call you back to ask questions because he might not. If he has any unanswered questions lurking in his mind and there is something he does not UNDERSTAND, your customer Mr. Reebuck will be less likely to take action.

If you need people to fill out an application, make sure the form is easy to complete and *looks* easy to complete. How many forms have you avoided just because they look intimidating or time-consuming? If at all possible, walk your audience through the forms so you can air out any questions or concerns. If you are asking people to go on-line for something, make sure your Web site is easy to navigate. Why not take them to your site before you leave and bookmark it for them. If there isn't time for that, then why not just e-mail them the link. Convenience closes lots of sales. If you need to arrange credit, make sure to explain why people need to fill out application forms; some people don't sign credit applications simply because they do not UNDERSTAND why they need to fill them out, and in particular, why you need *them* to do so.

I went into a high-end stereo store a few weeks ago and asked the salesperson about a sound system that was on display. He was quite helpful in explaining the system to me, carefully asking how and where I listen to music. But when it came time to discuss next steps, he slipped up. Because of the size of the system, I told the fellow I needed to measure the unit to make sure it would fit in the space I had in mind for it. Since I lived around the corner I figured I could return to pick it up within an hour.

Now, Schwartz is big on service. Schwartz gets turned off when service is lousy. Make no mistake; there is a big connection between service and sales. If you were this salesperson and a customer with "Buying Signals" written all over his face says that he needs the measurements to make a decision, what would you do? You would most likely get a measuring tape and measure the unit for Mr. Schwartz and then write those measurements on the back of your business card so that Mr. Schwartz wouldn't have to go looking for your number if he had any more questions. Mr. Schwartz would also remember your name which is a good thing considering that you are on commission. I wish you were my salesperson that day because that's not what this fellow did. I know it's hard to believe anyone would leave money on the table like that but he did. Big time. The salesperson handed me a tape measure and his card and walked away.

What's wrong with this picture?

Absolutely. He left it to me to do the measuring when he should have made my life easier by doing it for me. "Did he give you a pen," you ask? No he did not. Not only was I supposed to measure the unit myself, but also I was supposed to bring my own pen to the store. How silly of me to forget. So silly of me in fact that I ended up forgetting about the sound system altogether.

To make sure that your next steps are customer friendly, take a moment to answer the following questions. Let's call it an investment in preventive medicine.

What do you typically ask people to do as a next step(s)?

. . . .
. . . .

Where is there potential for confusion, delay or procrastination?

. . . .
. . . .

How can you make your next step(s) easier for the customer to act on?

. . . .
. . . .

When you close on the commitment to go the next

step, you might actually have several "next steps" in your sales cycle before you go to the Final Close. This is the moment after the need has been agreed to, your customers feel that your solution will take them to where they want to go, all questions/objections have been managed and there are no further obstacles to the sale. The road is clear to sign the deal or make the payment. The number of next steps may depend on how complex or expensive the sale is. If you are selling a water filtration system, people can make a quick decision. But if you are selling furniture, people may have to go back to their homes or offices to measure (a next step), or if you are dealing with an interior designer this person might need to consult with a client first (a next step). Suppose your average sales cycle requires that you have five meetings with your prospect before they are ready and able to make a purchase. At the end of each one of those meetings you have to secure permission to go to the next step or else your next meeting will not take place and the sale will never happen. So in this example you technically have five closes: the first four to get your prospect to book the next meeting, and in the final meeting you have a final close where the only next step is the purchase itself.

You will need many next steps if you are making a strategic sale. That's when your product has the potential to change the way a company does business, much like selling a new software application. Your buying cycle will take longer because a lot of people will need to UNDERSTAND your product and its impact on their organization. They will have to be ready, willing and able to accept the changes to their organization that your product will create. In this scenario, the initial person you are meeting may not be a decision maker, but rather someone who will influence the decision maker. While it's always preferable to deal with the person who is able to make the sale happen, influencers appear often and they have to be able to sell you internally to others. If you are dealing with this scenario, you might have to meet with several people to find out their needs and obtain their buy-in before a deal is done. (You could be facing as many next steps as a climb up an Aztec temple.)

Whether you have one next step or ten, make sure to articulate them in a clear, concise manner because if your audience does not UNDERSTAND what you want them to do next, they won't do it. (They might smile politely and say they will take the next step but you won't hear from them again.) You will find it helpful to visualize your next steps before walking into a sales call. This will enable you to focus on where you need to take your audience, and since you move in the images you create, whatever you focus on is the direction you will be headed.

It's always a good idea to get your customers to commit to something no matter how small that commitment is. For example, if you need to see someone again, book that meeting right then and there. I do that in my conference calls as well. Instead of saying, "I'll call you next week," I book the time right away. It is a form of commitment and every little commitment builds nicely to the big commitment of the final sale. After my initial sales call, I often ask my prospective customers to read some material which we will need to discuss in our next meeting, or I direct them to certain sections of my Web site. I honestly need them to UNDERSTAND this information, but I find that by formally making the review of material part of our next agenda, the commitment is more real for my audience. By the way, you might make a commitment of some kind to your customers; for example you might promise to call them at a certain time or you might promise to send them some samples etc. It's an easy way to build trust because you can demonstrate your ability to keep commitments.

If someone is sitting on the fence and cannot seem to commit, you might ask the person either, "Why can you not proceed?" or, "Is there any other information I can give you to help you make a decision?" If you suspect that the prospect is harboring a common objection that has not been communicated, be proactive: "Mr. Schwartz, are you unsure about the upgraded kitchen counter tops because you are concerned about scratching?" If that happens to be my concern, at least it is out in the open and you can deal with it with an effective response, which you would have prepared ahead of time (and perfected over time) in your Question/Objection Portfolio.

On those occasions when you simply cannot obtain permission to proceed to the next step, make sure you know why. There can be dozens of reasons. Take a second and write down what you experience most often:

What are the reasons why you do not close?

. . . .
. . . .
. . . .

Look at what you wrote and ask yourself if the reason why you did not close was because of something you did or something that was out of your control that had to do with the customer, or if it was for reasons unknown. Since I don't know what you wrote above, allow me to supply a few examples to augment your list. You might not close because of a timing issue; the customer does not need your product right away or is not ready to take delivery of your product right now. Perhaps you did not ask for the order. There might have been a question that was unasked, unanswered or both. It might be a delivery issue. (I couldn't buy a really nice large wooden wine rack once because I couldn't fit it in my car.) Maybe you were not speaking with the decision maker. It might be that you did not clearly articulate what was unique about your product or service. Could it be that there was no sense of urgency or you forgot to talk about What's at Stake? Did you have all the information you needed to complete your proposal? Sometimes you just don't have the right solution. Or could it be an issue of cost? Surprise. Surprise.

Price is a big one that you can't do much about unless you have flexibility in the price you offer and are willing to negotiate. People often make price an issue because there is no perceived value. They are more likely to pay for something (even if it's more expensive) when they see the value, especially if what you are offering is unique in any way. Uniqueness builds the value proposition. If your hourly rate is fifty dollars more than your competitor's, be prepared to explain not the difference in price but the difference in value. If you are a consultant you know it always pays to have a clearly defined list of deliverables to show people what they are getting for their money.

One day I went with my friend Karen Freilick to help her pick out a leather couch. She spotted two she liked, and there was a considerable price difference between them. The design of each was equal in appeal, so why the difference in price? The salesperson did not wait for Karen to ask. The woman explained to Karen the difference in the quality of the leather. Leather is leather, right? Not so. Some leather is soft, and some harder. Some lasts longer than others. The key was finding out what was important to Karen. Did she want the softer leather, which felt nicer, or the thicker leather that was more durable and would last longer? The salesperson asked Karen how much traffic she expected on the couch (I believe the qualifying question was, "Do you have children?") and the result was that Karen needed the more durable leather. Softer leather can be more expensive than other leather, but in this case it was not. Karen went with the thicker, more expensive leather couch because it better matched her needs. The value was clear. The sale was made.

When you explain the value, try leveraging what you learned when you Framed the Pain. For example, "Steven, you told me a half-hour ago that you need to sell your house in the next thirty days, and when you need to move a property that quickly it has to look its best because you can't afford to miss a single opportunity. That's why I am recommending that you repaint the whole house and not just the downstairs." (Notice how I also increased the sense of urgency by mentioning that the sale of the house had a time limit.) Remember to use the customer's own words and terminology.

If price remains an issue even after your audience clearly understands the value, consider adding more value rather than lowering the price. Throw in something extra. If you are selling office furniture, offer to come to the person's home or office and help them arrange it properly. If you are selling a scarf, which is being considered as a birthday present for someone, offer to gift-wrap it for free. If you are training a sales force, offer to provide more detailed feedback to the management on each participant's performance, including areas that will require ongoing support.

As your sales cycle progresses from one call to the next (including any telephone conversations), remember to stay connected with your audience because it only takes one disconnect in or between any sales call to lose the contract. This means that no matter how many sales calls you have with a person, never stop reading your audience or verifying what you heard. Make sure that your audience will UNDERSTAND and RELATE to what you say in each and every encounter. In this way you ensure that your prospect will be committed to each next step.

Also make sure your audience understands exactly the actions agreed upon. There are times when someone is required to take certain actions before the next meeting, such as send you information or speak with other colleagues etc. If there is any confusion after your sales call as to who is responsible for what, then you risk having your next meeting cancelled because your prospect is not prepared. Even if you go ahead with your next meeting it might not be as productive as it needs to be because someone did not come with important information they were supposed to gather. The solution is simple. At the end of your sales call, review the decisions that have been made, along with who has to do what and when. Write all this down to help those in your audience who are not good at taking notes. This not only reduces miscommunication but also acts as an action plan for everyone to reference. An action plan is yet another form of commitment.

At the beginning of every subsequent sales call, set the agenda as you learned in your third Island of Structure (Tune Your Audience In). New people might be dealing with you in the middle of your sales cycle and they too must be "Tuned In." At the end of each meeting, book the next sales call before you leave, regardless of whether you will be meeting again in person or following up on the phone. No matter how many next steps you have, your job is to keep up the momentum.

Can you RELATE to this scenario:

After a successful sales call, someone is very keen on what you are proposing and you agree to speak in a week. Then the customer calls to reschedule your next meeting but you are not in, so you're left a message. You call back but nobody's in, so you leave a message ... (you know where this is going). Before you know it a month goes by and you both have not met and the original enthusiasm or sense of urgency has died down—and with it the funeral has been arranged for your sale.

Whenever you need to speak with your prospective customer on the phone—to arrange meetings with other individuals or to answer questions or for a host of other reasons—*avoid leaving voice mail messages.* Telephone tag is one of the biggest killers of deals. It takes all the wind out of your sales momentum.

Another way to make sure that you stay connected with your prospects between meetings is to identify and eliminate any roadblocks to closing your final sale. The good news is that you can do this by applying a very simple test after each sales call.

Island 9
Test

Once you get a commitment to proceed to the next step, you will have to test the strength of that commitment. How many times have you arranged a second meeting with someone only to later have the meeting cancelled? The person lost interest, someone else got involved and decided not to proceed, internal politics got in the way, you had an undetected disconnect from your audience that came back to haunt you, or maybe it was any number of hidden barriers that sabotaged the deal.

Once you secure the right to go to the next step, take control and make sure it's going to happen. There is a very simple, subtle technique I'm going to recommend called The Test, which will do the trick. It must be carried out precisely, as I'm about to outline for you.

This technique kicks in once a meeting is completely over. You'll know it's over because the briefcases are being closed, and people are gathering their materials and getting up to leave. The reason why you have to wait until this very time is, that unless the meeting is absolutely over beyond a shadow of a doubt, people are still in "meeting mode," and on the defensive side because they know that they are in a sales call. But once a meeting is over, the defenses go down. The archers put away their bows and arrows and the drawbridge lowers. At this point anything you say will be viewed more casually.

Here's what you do: turn to the decision maker and ask something as straightforward as, "Has this meeting met your expectations?" That's all there is to it. Don't say another word. Just wait for a response and listen very carefully to the answer.

A quick note here: the question I just put forward is only a suggestion. In the spirit of what you are trying to accomplish, by all means ask what you are comfortable asking. A few variations would include: "Was this what you expected?" "Did you get all the information you needed?" "Did we cover everything?" "How do you feel about the meeting?" "Do you have any questions at all?" "Do you have everything you need?"

The answers you get back may or may not be what you expect to hear. Let's run through a few possible scenarios:

You: Was this what you expected?
Prospect: Yes, everything's fine.

Assuming this is an honest remark, you now know that there are no hidden roadblocks between you and that next step. As a bonus, you made your prospect feel good about the meeting because that person just told you that she received value for the time invested with you.

You: Did we cover everything?
Prospect:

> Yes. Everything's fine. We particularly liked your
> presentation, especially when you made us calcu-
> late the amount of potential business we over-
> looked.

In this kind of scenario you are told specifically about
what that person enjoyed about your sales call. This information enables you to gain a better insight into where you
are making an impact so you can leverage that in future
sales calls to other prospective customers. For example, if
someone tells you they liked a particular demonstration
you gave, you might think to take more time with this part
of your presentation in future.

You: How do you feel about the meeting?
Prospect:

> I was really impressed with your service guaran-
> tee. You are the first company to offer us anything
> that extensive.

If you are lucky, people might tell you what they
thought was unique about your company. That's a big
bonus. Many people find it difficult to know where they
are different, for the simple reason that they are too close
to it all. I remember an initial meeting I had with a well-
respected VP of training who told me that he had never
seen a learning model as deep as the one I had shown
him. That was the first time I'd heard such a thing, and considering the credibility of the source, I took the compliment seriously. I made a point after that of listening closer
to how other people responded to my learning model
and, lo and behold, they too offered similar observations. I

asked people why they thought my learning model was unique, and then I used their very remarks in my conversations on other sales calls when discussing this subject. Your unique selling proposition can also be leveraged in your telemarketing script and for use in handling objections, whether on the phone or in person.

You: Do you have everything you need?
Prospect:
          I think our group is fine for now, but you know,
          the person you will need to impress is Don down
          the hall. He's going to have some concerns over
          the timing issues we discussed.

In this scenario you just unearthed a hidden roadblock to the sale. Guess who your next meeting is going to be with? Let's get Don on the phone...

You: Was this demonstration what you expected?
Prospect:
          Not really. I still don't know how to use all the
          optional features.

So much for all the positive feedback. What happens, when people tell you the meeting fell short of their expectations? I've had many clients shocked the first time this happened, but they knew it was useful information. If people tell you they are unhappy for any reason whatsoever, you have a priceless opportunity right then and there to remedy the situation in real time. In fact, hearing your customers express how they feel in their own words will make their disappointment more real to you and give you a greater sense of urgency to act on it.

A client named Alexander had an experience with The Test that is worth sharing. One day he went to see an existing customer about getting a four per cent rate increase on two product lines. Attending the meeting was the general manager and one of his colleagues. The general manager said he could not go along with the proposed increase and if asked to do so he would be forced to take his business to a competitor. The general manager left and that was the end of the meeting. Alexander asked the general manager's colleague, "So what did you think about the outcome of this meeting?" She responded that the firm could take the four per cent increase on only one of the product lines. (Notice that Alexander did not specifically ask about rates; he asked the customer how she felt the meeting had gone and she volunteered to talk about rates.) That insight gave Alexander the ability to adjust his sales proposition so that one of the lines would get only a two to three per cent increase. The result was an agreement for an overall three per cent increase on the current $200,000 worth of business. Alexander noted that beyond the increase he secured, he retained the account!

The Test is not just for meetings. It's great for speeches and seminars. There are always people approaching you after a performance. That's a terrific opportunity to ask what part of your presentation made the biggest impact, what people found most helpful or what was the most unusual insight. Just two weeks ago I was giving a one-hour talk at the Schulich School for Business for the MBAs, and I had invited a couple of senior VPs I was "pitching" to come along as my guests. After the seminar I asked them separately the following question, "If there was one insight that made the biggest impact, what would it be?" They both told me what struck them most, and both answers were totally unexpected. This gave me invaluable insight into what was important to each person. As we said before, what's important to your audience is important to you. Make a list of what's important to your customers and then prioritize the entries. Whatever is at the top of the list will be on the top of your proposal.

When you know where you are scoring points with your audience you will be sure to build on those areas and enhance them with other examples or demonstrations or audience participation. It's also a great confidence booster just knowing that you are coming up to a part of your presentation where your audience will be listening to your every word and thinking, "WOW!"

After each sales call, self assess why people are either happy or not happy with your meeting or presentation. Leverage what you do well and remove any barriers that put your business opportunity at risk. Look for those issues which are in your control to fix, and then correct them right away so they don't reoccur in your next meeting. It's important to apply The Test after every sales call because you cannot afford even one disconnect. By applying The Test consistently you will keep your relationship constantly moving forward.

Presentations

Island 10
Presentations

As your sales calls progress you will need to make any number of presentations. What might begin as an answer to "Tell me about your services" later evolves into a more detailed discussion about a particular solution, one which addresses a customer requirement that has been identified and verified. At the final stage of your sales cycle you might walk your customer through a quote or detailed proposal. Presentations cannot be left to chance. They can either connect you with your audience and allow people to UNDERSTAND and RELATE, or they can cause a disconnection if your meaning is not crystal clear. Presentations are so common they often don't get the attention they deserve. When prepared and executed with precision, this Island of Structure will give you a tremendous amount of control over the outcome.

At any given point in your sales call you may be called upon to give a presentation. When I began implementing this system for my corporate clients I quickly discovered that people have all kinds of notions of what a presentation is. So I think that defining a presentation is a good place to start. Let's see what your impressions are. Take a second to answer this little quiz.

What is a presentation?

. . . .

Are presentations formal or informal?

. . . .

What are the average number of people in a presentation?

. . . .

What is the average length of time of a presentation?

. . . .

What kind of rooms are presentations held in?

. . . .

From my experience, any time you are communicating ideas or information you are giving a presentation, whether in person or over the phone.

When someone asks you to talk about your company, you are giving a presentation.

When a person at a social gathering asks, "So, what line of business are you in?" you are giving a presentation.

When someone asks you to explain one of your ideas, you are giving a presentation.

When you talk about a solution,
you are giving a presentation.

When you explain your products or services,
you are giving a presentation.

When you are giving a demonstration
of a product or service,
you are giving a presentation.

When you are walking someone through a process,
you are giving a presentation.

When you are showing your portfolio or
samples of your products,
you are giving a presentation.

When you are submitting a proposal in person,
you are giving a presentation.

Many people think presentations are all formal, such as when you are on a stage standing behind a podium or addressing people around a conference room table with all kinds of audiovisual aids. Your audience knows that such a gathering is a formal presentation because it is the sole focus of the sales call. But a presentation can be informal as well. Informal presentations are often given in the early stages of your sales cycle—when you are networking, or in an initial sales call when your audience wants to know more about you, your company and its products etc. In some form or another you are always presenting either to inform, influence, persuade or bring about a decision.

You are probably unaware of how many informal presentations you give each day. These informal presentations lead to the formal presentations. In fact, if you don't do a good job with your informal presentations, you won't have a formal presentation to proceed to. If you ask me about a product and my description of it does not capture your interest, or you do not UNDERSTAND or RELATE to it, then you won't ask me to elaborate. But when your informal presentations get people saying, "Tell me more!" then you have opened the door to a more formal presentation of your offerings and you move closer to the final sale.

Suppose you and I just met in an initial sales call. Ten minutes into the conversation you say, "Steven, tell me a little bit about your company." Right there I will be giving a presentation. It will be informal because it is not the sole focus of our meeting, and I may or may not have any audiovisual aids at my disposal. My presentation could be just for you, or you could have invited any number of people to join our meeting. A presentation is a presentation, whether it has an audience of one or thousands. It can be as short as a few minutes or counted in hours. It can be indoors in offices, homes or theaters or it could be outside in a parking lot. In short, a presentation can occur anywhere for anyone for any length of time.

What elevates a presentation beyond the art of conversation are the elements of structure and delivery.

A presentation is planned in a specific sequence and flows with carefully chosen words and phrases and perhaps some visuals, all of which are designed and tested to deliver a positive result. So if you were to ask me to tell you about my company, I would leave nothing to chance. I would know exactly what to say and would have perfected my patter over time so I would know that my presentation will make you WANT TO hear what I have to say and motivate you to open up the conversation.

The purpose of presenting is to communicate information so people will UNDERSTAND, RELATE and be in a better position to make a positive buying decision.

Presenting also means that you are not just giving information, but delivering information also. If you ask me for information on my services and I e-mail it to you, then I am only giving you that information. But if I call you on the phone after sending it and walk you through the material, then I am delivering that information. It's that personal delivery which defines your presentation. So even if your words are carefully chosen, they have to be delivered effectively to have full impact. Your presentation can sound as formal or informal as you like, but the content is always planned, rehearsed, tested and perfected over time.

Last month I walked into my favorite grocery store. I asked someone working there where I could find halvah, which is a delicious, sweet Middle Eastern dessert made of sesame paste. The sales clerk could have just said "aisle five" like other grocery store clerks would do, but that's not why I go to this specific store. The fellow walked me over to the aisle, but the halvah was not there. He went and collected some of his colleagues and before I knew it there were three of them looking for my halvah. Now that's what I call service. It turned out that the halvah had been moved to the cheese section. Now here's why I'm mentioning this story. The sales clerk didn't just take me to the halvah and give it to me and walk away. With great enthusiasm he gave me a little presentation on what made this particular brand unique, and even talked briefly about how it is made, which I found most interesting and educational. He knew his product and spoke with passion. Those are the makings of all great presentations.

It doesn't matter whether you are presenting product

samples, a portfolio or whether you are giving a formal three-hour presentation or a speech for that matter, your presentation has to be planned, constructed, polished, practiced, and fine-tuned—every time you deliver it until it is perfect. (Perfection is defined here as the state in which your presentation delivers on your objectives every time, leaving you with the greatest confidence in your ability to present.) When you go out there with a proven presentation, presenting becomes a lot more fun. As it should be.

I remember when I began my career in advertising, some of the other account executives in the agency where I worked were less than thrilled at the idea of approaching our clients with bold new ideas. I on the other hand was happier than a kid in a candy store whose mother leaves and says, "I'll be back in a few minutes." I loved presenting because I love what I do and I believe in the ideas I was presenting.

My performing background made me instinctively realize that when you are presenting to someone you have an audience, and when you have an audience, you have a show, and when you have a show you are giving a performance. A command performance: one that is memorable, engaging and energetic.

But effective presentations do not exist in a vacuum. If at any point prior to your presentation you somehow manage to disconnect from your audience, and as a result your audience tunes out, your presentation will never stand a chance because it will not be heard. That's precisely why I waited until now to discuss your presentations. Now that you know how to create an environment to close where you connect with your audience and stay connected, you now have an environment in which people will WANT TO LISTEN to your presentation.

Great presentations are no coincidence. They are built

for success from the ground up. I've had many clients tell me that they take a presentation and throw it against the wall a hundred times hoping that one day it will stick. Your success should not be guided by whim but by planning. Planning is the basis of control, and control is the foundation of confidence. (When was the last time you were out of control and confident?)

The objective here is to give you the tools and process to create effective presentations and test their effectiveness so you can keep improving them until they are flawless. This system will also deliver productivity gains, since it will take you less time to prepare your presentations.

There are five areas to address when looking to create effective presentations:

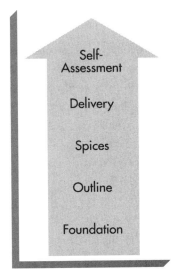

- **Foundation** is how you plan the content.
- **Outline** is how you put a plan into action, creating content that motivates people to take action.
- **Spices** are the theatrical devices that captivate your audience.

- **Delivery** brings content to life.
- **Self-Assessment** is the process by which content and delivery are tested and perfected.

While all five areas will be covered in our discussion, the main focus will be on planning and content because, without any real substance, there is nothing of value to deliver. How many times have you seen a presentation with great graphics but then walked away either not understanding what was said or not getting the information you needed? How many times have you heard someone speak who was incredibly dynamic but again you were left with no substance?

Content is king.

Very often people create a presentation for themselves and forget that the presentation is not about them at all. A good presentation is prepared to please your audience and is written from *their* perspective. Preparing one is similar to how good hosts plan a dinner party to accommodate their guests. Here, I'll show you...

Think about the next dinner party you are throwing. By the way, thanks for the invite. I have to admit that I love food and a dinner party is just a great excuse for great friends and great conversation, but above all, great food! To show how much I appreciate the invitation, I'll give you a hand planning the dinner.

Let's start with the basics:

✓ Who is coming to dinner?
✓ How many people?

Is Shira coming? You know Shira loves chocolate so she'll go nuts when you serve your famous walnut-fudge brownies. No wait, Paul can't have any. He has that nut allergy. Better stick with your chocolate cake. If Oliver is coming remember how he loves spicy food. Everyone's into garlic; so let's use fresh garlic and plenty of it.

- ✓ How many courses?
- ✓ What are the dishes you want to prepare?
- ✓ In what order should they be served?
- ✓ How spicy is it going to be?
- ✓ How is the food going to be presented?

Planning your presentation is not unlike this. Based on what you know about your dinner guests (your audience), you can plan what you are going to serve (the content), in what order and how it is presented. You also plan a highlight of the evening where your signature dish has friends talking for weeks. At the end of any dinner party you always fish for feedback to make sure everyone was happy. That's when you learn what dishes were a hit (especially if it's the first time you served them) and which ones need some refinement on the spices or the sauces.

I'm getting hungry just thinking about it. On with the show...

Foundation

Many years ago my dear Uncle Butch Farber in Montreal taught me a valuable lesson for the building of success. As we walked down a winding street to pick up a mouth-watering croissant and café au lait, he told me, "Steven, building a business is like building a house. If you want to build a house to live in, you have to have a strong foundation." The foundation he was referring to was a financial foundation, one in which you owned a home debt-free and had some money for cash flow so you could sleep at night. After you had that foundation in place you had a better chance of saving money, plus the advantage of having an asset to borrow money against should you need to invest in yourself. I followed my Uncle Butch's advice and, as always, it was right on the money.

That lesson was later taken to heart when I began to create presentations. You always build on a strong foundation. The one I want you to consider for your presentations works in three parts.

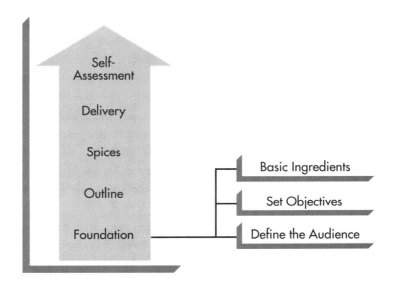

Each step is a building block. What you know about your audience helps define your objectives (objectives allow you to measure success), and what you know of your audience and your objectives gives you the essential ingredients that make your presentations successful.

Now, before we begin, think about an upcoming presentation (formal or informal) that you will be giving soon. At the end of each step of the process I have left a place for you to add your own material so you can build your presentation as you go along. By the time you work through this section, you should have all the pieces of your presentation ready to be drafted in final form, then delivered, tested and perfected.

Define the Audience

1. Number of people:

Even though you might have booked your meeting with one person, find out from the prospect or their assistant or colleague if there are any other people attending. The number of people will determine the size of the room and equipment you use. For example, if there are only three people you could use your PC to show some slides, but if there are six you would either need a screen or handouts. This is not to say that if six people showed up you would need six handouts. You might deliberately plan on three handouts so that sets of two get to share (enhancing participation). It also never hurts to have a few extra handouts just in case someone unexpected shows up. Be prepared.

Knowing how many people you are presenting to also helps you prepare mentally for your performance and by doing so, keeps you in control. Before I go into any meeting, seminar or speech, I always want to know the size of my audience so I can prepare myself for it. I do this by visualizing myself sitting in the audience looking at someone who is giving the presentation, and in fact it's me up there. Placing myself for a moment in the role of the audience allows me to view how people will see me, how the lighting and sound affects them, and how the general ambience of the room makes them feel. I'm more relaxed when I commence the presentation.

The number of people you are expecting: . . . .

2. Industry:

From what industry is your audience? I know this sounds terribly basic, which it is, but the reason why you should always list the industry is so you have a visual reminder of where your presentation needs to be focused. If today you are going to do a presentation about your company to someone in the transportation industry, and tomorrow you will be talking with someone in the manufacturing industry, you should invest the time to tailor your message to your audience. This might entail only a small adjustment, but it could make a significant difference. Since your audience has to UNDERSTAND and RELATE to what you have to say, your words will have to reflect the issues and jargon of the industry your audience works within so that you activate their Greed Glands, and by doing so secure its undivided attention.

Industry: . . . .

3. Position:

There are two areas to look at here. One is to identify whether your prime contact is a decision maker or an influencer (a person who can influence a decision maker). If it's the latter you will need to adjust your presentations and handouts so they are easy for influencers to present internally to others at a later date. The second area to address is the actual role your client plays in the organization. I always like to know the mindset of the audience I'm addressing. A VP has different issues than a CEO, and someone in charge of training has different needs than someone in charge of sales. A homeowner has different concerns than someone who is renting. I can use the position of the person I'm speaking with as a reference to make sure that whatever my message is and whatever examples I give incorporate the same language as my audience.

There was a time a few years back when understanding the mindset of my audience came in real handy to secure a hotel room. May I share this story with you? Great! My associate Rod and I are attending a conference in Atlanta, which is hosted at one of the big hotel chains. Prior to going down I had called up and specifically booked a non-smoking room, since I have an allergy to cigarette smoke. To accommodate Rod's schedule we had arranged an evening flight from Toronto, arriving late at night, way past the bedtime of an early riser like me. (I'm not a happy camper when I'm up past my body clock.) That said, I drag my tired butt over to the check-in counter and ask for my room. The good news is they have my reservation. The bad news is they have not booked a non-smoking room. No matter what I said they will not give me the room they promised because, they claimed, there are no non-smoking rooms available.

Too tired to argue any further I take the keys and head up to my room. In the elevator I ask Rod if he wants me to arrange a non-smoking room for him in the morning and he says no, since smoke doesn't bother him in the least. He came to regret his decision.

I am up all night because the smell of stale smoke in the room is making me nauseous. After my morning coffee I approach the attendant at the front desk and tell her to make sure a non-smoking room is reserved for me by the time I get back at 5:00. The person just smiles and asks if I can come back every hour to see if one becomes available. "Why would I do that?" I ask, grinding my teeth which my dentist tells me is not a good thing to do. "I have just traveled a thousand miles to attend a convention your hotel is hosting and I'm not leaving that convention just to see if you have a room that you promised me in the first place. You have a computer. When the room becomes available just book me in. Thank you."

At lunch time I come back to check in on the progress. You are ahead of me here; yeah you're right, still no room. How did you know? As Popeye used to say just before he tore into his spinach, "This is all ize can stands cuz I can't stands no more!" I tell Rod to wait five minutes before we go off for lunch.

"What are you going to do?" he asks, knowing the answer.

"I'm going to get my room," I reply, heading for the house phones.

For the next few minutes I stop and collect my thoughts. I want to speak with the decision maker, who I figure is the owner of the hotel. I somehow know instinctively that what I need to do is construct how I am going to present my case to this hotel owner so I don't come across like some complaining spoiled little guest. (As you have correctly observed, what I was preparing was an informal presentation, even if it was over the phone. The goal was to persuade my audience to recognize my needs as a hotel guest and give me my room.)

I have to move quickly to prepare the storyline. I think about the mindset of my audience and what issues are important to him. I put myself in the owner's shoes. If I ran an upscale hotel, I'm thinking, then poor service would be my biggest nightmare because I'd risk turning off my guests. All my efforts would be toward steering my staff to move to a high level of service. Once I figure this out I quickly take out a pen and pad and script what I am going to say, and then I do a quick rehearsal once the coast is clear and there is no one standing beside me on the other house phones. Then I pick up the phone for the moment of truth.

"Can I help you?" the operator says in the same dry tone she must have used a thousand times all morning.

"I'd like the name of the person who owns the hotel please."

"That would be Mr. Garrett. I'll put you through."

Ring. Ring. Ring.

"Mr. Garrett's office. How can I help you?"

"Is Mr. Garrett the owner of the hotel?" I verify.

"Mr. Garrett is the manager."

"I need to speak with the *owner* of the hotel."

"That would be Mr. John Taylor. Would you like me to put you through to the executive office?"

"Yes please" I say, using up the last of my Canadian politeness.

Ring. Ring. Ring.

"Mr. Taylor speaking."

"Mr. Taylor, we haven't been introduced before, my name is Steven Schwartz. I'm a guest at your hotel."

"How can I help you Mr. Schwartz?"

"Mr. Taylor, you are the captain of a ship, and as a captain of a ship you want to make sure that your ship lands at the destination you charted. Well, I'm here to tell you that the crew you have hired down below is rowing in a completely different direction from where you want this ship of yours to go."

Well, at this point the fellow is all-ears as I tell him the story of what happened.

To make a long story short, he apologizes for what happened, arranges for a non-smoking suite for me, and when I get there at 5:00 in the afternoon there is a huge basket of fruit with a very fine bottle of wine from Mr. Taylor's private cellar. Most impressive is the one-page handwritten note, which he sent to thank me for pointing out where his ship was headed. He signed it, "The Captain."

What made my presentation persuasive was a combination of factors: there was the planning, preparation and rehearsing. I was dealing with the decision maker. There was the fact that I came across as a friend offering some advice rather than being confrontational. But let's not forget that Mr. Taylor was able to UNDERSTAND and totally RELATE to my message because I understood his position and could speak his language and hit his Greed Glands by zeroing-in on an issue near and dear to his heart: the direction his ship was headed.

It shows you just how short, informal and persuasive a presentation can be.

Position: . . . .

4. Audience Expectations:

When you meet someone either for the first time or for a subsequent meeting, you more than likely will be facing a series of expectations that you created in your last conversation. You need to make note of what these are or else how can you deliver on them? Think back to your telephone sales call or your last visit with your customer. How did you close? How did you end the meeting? Did you ask to see your prospect to demonstrate something? Did you agree to meet to discuss a specific issue or need? Is the person expecting you to come with certain information? Is she expecting this to be a fact-finding meeting or something more tangible? Whatever is expected, you have to make good on.

Do you remember the earlier story of my insurance agent Charles? At the end of our conversation Charles said that he would see me the next day after doing his homework and working out exactly what policy was best for me. Charles obviously made note of what I was expecting because, as you know, he delivered.

Clients might have asked you to read through their annual report before coming, and if so you better believe they'll be asking you about it. I was once getting ready for a second meeting with prospective clients when I received a phone call from my associate, Paul Mosley, who gave me a heads up. "Steve-O, the prospects are expecting you to come in with a proposal. They want to cut to the chase." That was the first I heard of it. The prospects had not said anything about it, but after having a meeting with Paul, they were suddenly ready to move things forward and Paul correctly sensed that the company was moving fast. I put a formal quote together for the meeting and everything went just fine.

Expectations form a two-way street. You might ask your prospects to do something too. I often ask people to visit my Web site or peruse my book before our first meeting. I call ahead of time to make sure that they have had the time to review the site, and if they did not, then I simply reschedule the meeting. Sales calls are not for wasting time. They're for exploring opportunities.

Audience Expectations:

. . . .
. . . .
. . . .
. . . .

5. The number one issue affecting your audience:

As you know, when you address the main issue affecting your audience they UNDERSTAND and RELATE to your message. Centering your discussion on people's main issue, challenge or concern gives you the power to take control over their energy and focus. You hit their Greed Glands. You now command their undivided attention. If you have the answer to a problem, you will be listened to. In my hotel story a few minutes ago I was able to uncover the main issue affecting my audience (bad service affecting the hotel's reputation) because I had identified the position of my audience. I was aware that chief executives are responsible for the direction their companies are taking. I leveraged this fact to command the chief executive's attention. But a person's position is not the only indicator of the types of issues at hand. The issues can also be industry-specific (agriculture, plastics, manufacturing, financial, transportation, small business etc.). They can be issues of demographics, which you want to be aware of if you are targeting the elderly or early retirees. There can be issues specific to the amount of wealth one has: a person with millions has different issues than someone who is still accumulating. There are issues concerning the size of companies you are marketing to: start-up companies have different issues than established companies. The list goes on and on. By putting the main issue on your radar screen, you can reference it when you are ready to weave it into your message at various points in your presentation, and throughout your sales call for that matter.

Issue knowledge is also necessary when creating an effective script for your initial telephone sales call. Best of all, it gives you a tremendous advantage going into your meeting because it keeps you focused on what really matters. As you know, what's important to your audience is important to you.

Some issues you will know in advance by researching the company or industry you are addressing. (Visit Web sites, read industry journals, annual reports, newsletters, and speak with people in the industry you want to approach.) When you set the agenda in your initial sales call you will naturally refer to the issue that is top of mind with your audience. As your meeting progresses you will uncover more specific issues when you Frame the Pain and find out What's at Stake. (Frame the Pain should also confirm the primary issue.) If you hear that someone's concerns have changed or that they are simply different than those you had researched, then go with the issue your audience just articulated. Even though there is bound to be more than one issue, I need you to focus on the number one issue affecting your audience— because that's the one that your audience will respond to most strongly.

The number one issue affecting your audience:

. . . .
. . . .

6. Audience Jargon/Buzzwords:

You can't expect anyone to UNDERSTAND or RELATE to what you are saying if you don't speak the same language. I don't mean literally. When I wrote marketing materials for Nortel, I once explained to a VP: "Imagine what would happen if you put all your customers in a room and stood there reading your own brochures. Now imagine if you divided the room in half, with the "techies" on the left side and the non-technically minded business people on the other. If you stand there talking technical jargon you'll turn off the right side of the audience, and if you speak in a corporate tone you'll alienate the left side of the room. The answer would be to give two presentations—one for the techies and one for everyone else who does not UNDERSTAND technical jargon."

Get to know the audience's jargon or buzzwords so that you can UNDERSTAND them when they communicate with you, and you can be understood when you communicate with them. A simple example: when the World Wide Web came into being and people started talking about "surfing the Web." If you were speaking with a technology company in those early days of the Internet, you would either want to use that phrase in your conversation or at the very least be aware of it so you would UNDERSTAND your audience's use of such terms.

When you speak the same language you send a signal

that you UNDERSTAND their business, and this is a subtle yet powerful way of connecting with your audience. Your credibility goes up as a result and along with it you begin to build trust. When you use the language of your audience you bridge the gap between the presenter and the audience. You move from "YOU and THEM" to "US." You become one with the audience. This was just such the case a few years ago when I was giving a one-hour presentation at the Third Annual Forum on Private Equity Investing. I asked the person organizing the event what was top of mind for the audience. "Deal Flow," the organizer said. Bingo! Deal flow was their buzzword, and so I used it in the title of the presentation and in my opening line. It enabled me to connect instantly, and not just because they knew I spoke their language. Speaking in their terms helped me focus on my audience. In other words, I moved in the direction of the images I created.

I'm not suggesting that you ramble on using every industry buzzword. Just use a few selected ones in the right place at the right time for impact. For example, suppose part of your business jargon included talking about "partnering with customers" to build solutions. If you were presenting to someone in the recording business you would substitute "partner" with "collaborate," since that is the language common to the recording industry. So you'd end up saying, "We collaborate with customers to build solutions." That would send an instant message that you speak the language, and you'd make a good strong connection in just a matter of seconds.

To get a feel for how your audience speaks, take a look at the things they read and create, including their own presentation materials. If there is no jargon, or buzzwords to leverage, don't worry about it. If you are working with many different industries, keep a database of all the buzzwords of each market segment so you can refer to them quickly the next time you prepare a presentation.

Here's an interesting story about a time when I couldn't speak the language of my audience, but I spoke the language of *their* audience. Early in my advertising career I wanted to target the technology sector, but it was going to be a long shot because I did not speak their language. I could not read computer manuals and could not UNDERSTAND any of the technical jargon, which was most of what they spoke back then. I also knew that this lack of technical knowledge would be the number one objection any computer company would have in hiring me to write their marketing material. So the challenge for me was to figure out how to turn a weakness into strength.

And then it dawned on me.

I could not speak the language of the technology companies but I could speak the language of their customers, which was even more important. As it turned out, language communication was the biggest challenge facing technology companies. Most customers did not UNDERSTAND the technology and many people were intimidated by it, a matter made worse by the fact that many computer companies wrote much of their marketing materials in computer industry jargon which was not the language of choice for the majority of consumers at the time. So I made a telephone sales call to Hamilton Computer Sales and Rentals, which at the time was Digital's biggest distributor. I was sitting across from the VP of Marketing, Will Jenke. I showed him my threadbare portfolio, which did not contain any computer industry material. Will turned to me and said point-blank, "You don't know anything about computers." Without as much as batting an eye I replied, "Neither do your customers." He broke out laughing. I then went on to explain that if people are going to purchase computers they need to UNDERSTAND these products in everyday English, which is what I knew best. And because I could not UNDERSTAND his company's technical jargon, I knew audience would not either. But I knew how to communicate it in everyday language. Will hired me on the spot and thus began a long and prosperous working relationship with that industry.

Audience Jargon/Buzzwords:

. . . .

. . . .

7. *Audience Type:*

You should always adjust your presentation to match the personality style of your audience; otherwise you run the risk of disconnecting from them. You can find out in advance what type of person(s) you are presenting to, or you can pick up clues from their surroundings once you meet.

When I need to know what type of person I am presenting to, I often do research on them as part of my homework when preparing my initial telephone sales call. Once I've established a good rapport with someone's assistant I will often ask something like, "What type of person is Mary? (Prospect)." Sometimes I'll hear answers like, "Oh Mary is a real people person," or "She likes to read a lot of material, " or "She's very bright." I can also often catch a glimmer of insight from the prospect's voice mail. Call your prospects late at night or early in the morning before work begins so that and listen to their voice message. You can obtain mental images of people just from their voice. You can also pick up good information by listening to the way they speak; they might speak softly, they might have lots of energy and speak enthusiastically, they might talk at the speed of sound (Type A personality for sure) or they might speak very slowly (very methodical, perhaps the analytical type).

Once you meet your prospects you will have another opportunity to see what they are like.

If I go into someone's office and see a pile of books, reports and articles everywhere I will assume that the person is the analytical type. From my experience these are people who love to go into detail on just about everything, and they are not shy to ask for refills when it comes to asking questions. (You might want to refer back to the Reading the Audience section where we talked about how people reveal their personalities through the kinds of questions they ask.) Unless you provide these people with all the answers and all the details, they are not able to take action because they need all this information to UNDER-STAND your message. If you find yourself presenting to this type it is advisable to slow down so your audience can analyze your dialogue thought by thought. They are methodical and need to take their time carefully. Be prepared to walk slowly. I come prepared for the analytical types by keeping a detailed twelve-page document which explains my Learning Model in great detail. I use this as a leave-behind, which analytical people always appreciate. By the way, if I have never met the person I'm presenting to but I get the opportunity to speak on the phone, I make a point of mentioning that I have such a detailed document and if there is a quick request to see it, I know I have an analytical on my hands.

Have you ever had a meeting with someone who wanted nothing more than to ask you all kinds of questions about YOU for the first fifteen minutes: where you went to school, how you got into the business, how you like your work, what you do for fun, etc? These people are big on relationships, they are the ultimate "People, People." When I know that I'm dealing with people who are big on relationships, I budget a little extra time up front in the meeting so I can get to know them and vice versa. I also make sure to include the human element in any examples I present so this audience can see how people's lives are affected. If possible you should include in your presentation some descriptive examples of how other customers have benefited from your products or services.

Then there are those people who talk so fast you wonder if they spoke before the words even formed in their minds. Type A personalities also want you to get to the point and expect that everything that is said and shown should support a decision. Don't bog them down talking about other people, and whatever happens don't even dream of pulling out the long version of your presentation. Details might be hazardous to your health with this audience. Pick up the pace and stay very, very focused. I often keep a separate presentation for this group with visuals that help summarize what I'm discussing. For example, I use a single visual that sums up my whole system, and another visual snapshot that sums up my Learning Model. I make sure to give this audience a road map to every section so that they can sit and listen without wondering where the conversation is going.

My clients often ask me for the secret to holding the attention of Type A personalities (which I manage to do for even three-hour presentations). If Type A's are not stimulated every minute you risk disconnecting from them. (You know you have held their attention when everyone comes back after the break.) Here's the secret: give Type A people relevant information *every minute* so that every sixty seconds they are saying to themselves, "Wow, I didn't know that" or, "That's interesting." Make it fast-paced (which does not mean rushed) and entertaining as well. Whenever possible, get them doing something. Participation keeps their minds occupied.

You will never go wrong with Type A people and every other person on the planet you may be addressing if you follow this simple rule:

Talk about what's important to the audience.

When you do this, your audience will give you their undivided attention, and that in turn will energize you. It's not only a great feeling, but also a feeling of power to know you are in complete control of your audience. Your boost of energy only enhances the connection with your audience, since people are attracted to people who energize them.

Somewhere about now you noticed that I had not addressed the issue of what to do when there are different types of people all in the same room. My experience has taught me to come prepared to cover your bases. Have two versions of your presentation at all times: version A for Type A personalities who want the *Reader's Digest* style and then a regular presentation with the normal amount of detail and a few customer stories but with some extra information (handouts, back-up charts, slides) in your hip pocket just in case the analytical types show up.

Audience Type:

. . . .

Set Objectives

1. Length of presentation:

In order to finish on time you need to determine the length of your presentation. You'll want to tell your audience so they can measure their time and attention span accordingly, especially the Type A people. So the obvious question is: how long is your presentation? Well, how long does it really need to be? If someone gives you twenty minutes to present an idea people tend to take the whole twenty minutes. However, if you can present your idea, in ten, why drag it out? People's time is the only non-renewable resource they have, and most people like to use it wisely. So what I suggest is that when you first sit down to create your presentation, assume the presentation is the length of time you are given. Once you complete your presentation and are satisfied that it meets all your objectives, time it. If it's less than your original designated time, go with the shorter version. If anything, this allows you to leave more time for people to ask questions and open a meaningful dialogue. If it fits the time slot exactly, so be it. However, if your presentation takes longer than the time you have, you will have to find ways to make it shorter. If you have to cut it back, eliminate any content that is not outlined in the Basic Ingredients section, which you will be covering next.

If you feel strongly that you need more time, see if you can't get it by asking your prospects to extend your meeting, but be prepared to explain the value they'll receive for that extra investment in time. When I speak in front of large corporate audiences, I am sometimes asked if I can speak for twenty minutes. On every such request, I told the prospective client that my objective is to give the audience the information they need to feel confident enough to go out and apply the system. To do a proper job and cover all the material, I need one-hour at the very least, and it's a packed one-hour at that with not one ounce of fat. I simply will not speak for twenty minutes and leave half of the important material out. Because I demonstrate the value of the extra time, time my request for a longer presentation has always been granted.

As a former advertising copywriter I can tell you from experience that it's often harder to write a five-word slogan than it is to write a six-page brochure. If you only have five words to get your meaning across and capture the attention of your audience, you have no room for error. Precision is the name of the game. It's not so much about being economical; it's about carefully crafting words that have impact. In *How To Make Hot Cold Calls* I outlined a methodology for telling your story in thirty words or less. So no matter how short or long your presentation, choose your words carefully. Think about the images your words create in people's minds. The more meaningful and memorable those images, the greater the impact your presentation will have.

What I'm driving at is: it's not the length of the performance that counts—it's the quality of the performance. The impact. The length a presentation merely gives you the parameters for building one.

Length of Presentation:

. . . .

2. What you want the audience to do at the end:

If you don't know where you are going, how will you get there? If you are going to close on the commitment to take the next step, you should be clear in your mind as to what that next step is. You would be surprised how many people don't walk away with what they need simply because they did not ask. So let's look at what you need your customer to commit to at the end of your presentation.

At the end of an informal presentation where you are casually asked about your company or its offerings, your objective might be as simple as having people open up a dialogue and ask more detailed questions. You might want them to talk specifically about a certain aspect of your presentation. For example, after I tell people about my company the first thing I do is follow it with a discussion about their own challenges and experiences. If that has already been discussed, I encourage the conversation to direct itself toward training issues.

At the end of a formal presentation on something like a proposal, you are most likely at a close, a point where you want people to make a purchase or commit to a trial of your service. If it was the latter objective, then at some point in your presentation you might wish to plant the idea of a trial by talking about the experience other customers have had with your trial, and what's involved etc.

That way, by the time you get to the end of your presentation, the idea of a trial is already on the table.

If you are selling insurance and you need your prospective customer to fill out an application, you could mention the form in your conversation and then casually hold it up as you talk about it in passing. In this rather informal way you have flashed the application in front of your audience so that by the end of your presentation it will seem only natural to make the request to fill out the form.

The point is simply knowing what you want your audience to do at the end of your presentation so you can take the steps necessary to get there.

What you want the audience to do at the end:

. . . .

. . . .

3. What you want the audience to learn:

I once heard a slogan in a television commercial for a clothier that went, "An educated consumer is our best customer." The more people learn from your presentation, the better they will UNDERSTAND. When people learn, their thoughts become clearer. It gets them thinking and talking, asking questions that move the conversation forward. They might even learn something totally fascinating and be WOWED! In the process.

All you want to do at this point is identify the key learning points that either aid in that understanding or help people to see your value proposition. People can learn from facts and figures, answers to questions, hands-on demonstrations, or stories that reveal the experiences of others.

So what does your audience need to learn? Start by looking at anything they need to know in order to make a decision. Is there any technology, process or terminology they need to be aware of? Any guarantees? Perhaps an understanding of what is unique about your solution. If you were in the wine business you would certainly want me to know about the complexities of wine. If you were selling consulting services to a particular industry you might want your audience to develop a deeper understanding of some of the issues facing their industry that they were not previously aware of. In this way, you will build your stature as an authority whose services must be obtained.

For my own business the first and most important thing I want my audience to learn is the philosophy behind my systems, not only to help them appreciate the unique characteristics of my methods but also to help me qualify my audience. At the end of the day, if they do not share the underlying beliefs of my approach, they are not candidates for my systems. That's why I outlined the Fundamentals at the beginning of this book.

Suppose your company established a new computerized billing system so your customers could view, approve and pay invoices on-line. If you were presenting this new concept to your customers, I imagine that it would be important for them to know how to read the new electronic invoices and get acquainted with some of the important features of the system.

Have you ever visited a really good garden center in the spring? When you are looking at all the various flowers and plants, you can never know enough. The really good salespeople are the ones who take the time to explain every little thing about the plants: how much moisture is required, how much sun or shade and which type of sun (morning, midday or late afternoon), what plants grow well together and on and on. (If you get a Virgo like me talking about plants we'll be here forever.) The more you know, the easier it is to make a buying decision.

If your product is the result of a labor-intensive production process, people should know the work involved in its creation to appreciate its value. Last month I was in a car dealership and the salesperson took extra care to make sure that I knew how many coatings of paint that were applied and the special finish used. This made me appreciate what I was paying for in a car like that, and made me ask more questions as to what else was unique about the car.

To allow your audience to make a decision, give them what they need to know. That's assuming of course your audience is willing and able to digest all the necessary information. Read your audience to see if they are ready for more information. If the people you are addressing are either; analytical, very sharp, or very eager to ask questions that move the conversation forward, that's usually a good sign that they will WANT TO hear all of what you have to say. If you sense that your audience has had enough information, don't overload them. Information is like very rich food that should be given in small amounts. If it tastes good, some people will want more, assuming they're not counting calories.

What you want the audience to learn:

. . . .
. . . .

4. What you want the audience to experience:

One of the most effective ways to help people learn something is to have them experiences it by doing or observing something themselves. It's one thing to look at a car to study its features, but it's quite another to experience those features. It's called a test drive. If you sell fine leather goods, just have someone experience the leather by touching it. Feeling is believing. A winery on the other hand, has tastings where people smell and savor the complexities of the vintage.

Experience is all about playing on the senses.

I was at an upscale kitchen store where on display was every kind of high-quality olive oil and balsamic vinegar you could imagine. Company executives understood that customers could learn the difference between oils simply by speaking to their knowledgeable staff, but they also knew that the only way customers could learn how the products tasted was to experience them. So lots of samples were set out in little paper cups. But no tasting experience is complete without a little bread for dipping, so the bread was there too, cut up in just the right sizes for sampling. This not only resulted in the sale of a lot of oil and vinegar, it also got people into a different frame of mind and almost created a little party atmosphere in the olive oil section. The oils became an experience unto themselves.

If you are selling antiques, then what you want people to experience is the past. People who love antiques tend to love history, especially the history of their antiques. People are not only buying the antique, they are purchasing the history that comes with it. One of my prized pieces is a stunning wardrobe from the mid-eighteen hundreds made from Ontario pine. The person who sold it could have just shown it to me or answered my questions, but instead he brought it to life with stories of the people who owned the cabinet and the farm they lived on. By living through the history I was able to experience the cabinet on a different level.

So what might you need people to experience? If you are selling software you could have customers watch a demonstration to experience how easy it is to use; to be more memorable and convincing you could have them try out the software with their own hands. (Just be sure that you are speaking with the right audience. Some decision makers don't need to see demonstrations. People that influence decision makers will likely benefit from touching the merchandise. In any event, don't rely on demonstrations to carry the day for you. You still have to create the overall environment where people WANT TO buy from you.)

Suppose you are an architect and are talking to me about building a custom home. If you knew that I had a concern about completion time, what you would want me to experience is a certain comfort level in your ability to meet my expectations. That comfort level could be achieved by walking me through the whole process from design to construction and even landscaping. By demonstrating your knowledge of the process I would know that I'm in good hands.

What you want the audience to experience:

. . . .

. . . .

5. The overall impression you want to impart:

Impressions are planned. They are also created and enhanced throughout your presentations and your customer relationship.

Case in point: part of the impression you make relates to the shopping experience you are providing. Retail stores have long understood that aside from product, price and selection, success lies in the uniqueness and completeness of the overall shopping experience. Whether you are selling consulting, plumbing or window cleaning, the customer's experience has to be a positive and memorable one. If you were in the hotel business, you would know that the Ritz is not just a hotel, it's an experience defined by unparalleled service and attention to every single tiny detail. In any shopping experience, you can find Silver service, Gold service and the Platinum standard of excellence. What's yours?

If as an interior designer you were presenting ideas to me, the level of service you define for yourself will be reflected in your presentations. With each level of service the experience is enhanced. For example, if you were offering Silver service you might present the ideas in your office; the ideas could be detailed in a series of sketches and you might even have some fabric samples with you so that I can not only see them, but also touch them to appreciate the texture. If you offered the Gold standard you might present your ideas in my home; your sketches might have already been downloaded to my computer before you even arrive. You would probably give me a greater variety of samples to look at. If you were the Ritz of interior design, you might come to my home to present the ideas but take me to the stores where the very fabrics are already displayed, or whisk me off to where they are manufactured to enhance my learning and buying experience. You might even leave me with a tool to help me sort through my choice of materials.

Take a moment and define the experience of working with your company including how your service level will affect your presentation.

Platinum:

....
....
....
....

Gold:

....
....
....
....

Silver:

....
....
....
....

On a different level, there is always an impression you want to make that relates to a basic part of your selling proposition. For example, though every good interior designer has their own style (modern, traditional etc.) they need to leave the impression that they have the ability and flexibility to create a look that reflects the unique tastes and lifestyles of their clients. To illustrate this you could show customers examples of what you did for others, share your philosophy of what good design should be, and even discuss the kinds of suppliers you can access.

If you sell take-out pizza, the overall impression you might need to make, other than having great-tasting pizza, is that you have fast, reliable delivery. One way you could make a strong impression is by talking about your guaranteed delivery. If you were a consulting company and wanted to leave the impression that customer satisfaction was assured, you could talk about your money-back guarantee, your track record of customer satisfaction, or the processes you have in place to ensure customer satisfaction. My financial planner made sure during our first meeting that I left with the impression that he was very prudent with the investment decisions he makes for his clients. He did this by telling me of his chartered accounting background and explaining his conservative approach to investing.

If you are selling employment services, you want to leave the impression that the people you recommend are reliable, available and can do the job. If you were making a presentation on an end-to-end solution, you would need to leave the impression that you can look after your customer's needs from beginning to end.

If you are a freelance advertising copywriter or graphic designer, you want to leave the impression that you UNDERSTAND the business of your prospect—and you are highly imaginative. For my entire working career my business card has been a playing card with an ace of spades on one side which includes my company name and phone number. It is plastic coated with rounded corners so it looks and feels like a real playing card. On the back is my company logo. Nowhere does it say what I do, but it leaves the unmistakable impression that I am creative and unique. It is also very, very memorable. A VP approached me once who remembered my business card from ten years ago. Impressions are long-lasting indeed.

That's why impressions are so important. Whatever impression you make, knowingly or otherwise, people carry them in their minds throughout your sales cycle and throughout the customer relationship. Impressions can work for you to accelerate the buy decision or work against you to make your sales cycle longer or even jeopardize your ability to close. If my financial advisor had done anything to give me a different impression of him we would not have done business together.

Take a moment and pretend that the impression you want to make can actually come in a box which can be left behind with your audience after your sales call. Now picture someone opening that box and looking at your impression.

Describe what this impression of yours looks like:

. . . .

. . . .

. . . .

What would people say about it?

. . . .

. . . .

. . . .

Is it something people would want to show their friends?

. . . .
. . . .

Would they tell their friends about it? (Word of mouth is a beautiful thing.)

. . . .
. . . .

I was coaching a financial consultant named Stewart who was making presentations to senior citizens. The impression he wanted to make was that he cared about what was important to them. This fellow really did. One of the ways he would convey that image was by incorporating the phrase "Every penny counts." You see, most of the people Stewart was presenting to went through the Great Depression. Back then, when people said "every penny counts," they meant it. So at the right opportunity Stewart would mention how he too shared this philosophy, which instantly left the desired impression. One person Stewart saw actually told him before signing up, "You are the only person who ever said that to me." More important, Stewart adopted this expression as a personal credo that fashioned everything he did; it came out in the conservative approach he took to financial planning, it affected the way he watched out for portfolios, and it quietly translated into the respectful way he treated his clients—all enhancing the impression he wanted to make.

The overall impression you want to impart:

. . . .
. . . .
. . . .

6. How you want the audience to feel:

Sales have a lot to do with transferring a feeling. A good real estate agent can make you feel the spaciousness or brightness of a home. They can help you feel what it is like to live in that new home. They want you to see yourself living there. We move in the images we create, and if you can't see yourself living in that home, you won't buy it. Last weekend I walked through a beautiful estate in the township of Caledon, and this place had everything: three acres, lots of forest, two fireplaces, cathedral ceilings, a huge living room. You get the picture. As I walked through the house and the property I was not so much interested at first in all the detail, although that would come later. I was trying to picture myself living there. I could easily see myself enjoying the view off the solarium. It seems that I was not alone. Someone had just put in an unconditional offer the week before. They obviously shared the same feeling for the place. By the way, the vendors also want you to feel at home. If you walk in during an open house and you smell home-baked bread, it's no coincidence.

When you visit a clothing store you try something on because it looks nice. Hopefully it looks just as nice once you're wearing it. But how many times have you tried on some clothing and even though it looks good you don't feel good in it or you can't see yourself wearing an outfit like that. Last month I popped into a clothing store and tried on a jacket that caught my eye. It looked good and it fit just fine, but I couldn't see myself wearing it because I already own several other sports jackets. Then along came the salesperson who walked up to me with this beautiful shirt to wear with the jacket, and once I tried it on with the outfit I suddenly could see myself in a jacket like that, as long as it came with that shirt. I ended up buying five shirts with that jacket. (Call it a weakness.)

When I invite friends over for dinner they show up. That's because I don't just invite them; I sell them on the idea. I describe what's on the menu in mouth-watering terms until they feel hungry just listening to me, and run to get their calendars. If I'm inviting my chocoholic friends, the deal is closed when I describe the *smell* of my homemade chocolates.

It never hurts to make your customers feel good after they've made a purchase. Ever notice how good you feel when you come home with something you bought that was wrapped in fancy tissues?

Knowing how you want someone to feel also affects your tone. If you want someone to be excited about something, your energy level is going to be up there. If you want someone to feel relaxed, like when you walk into a health spa, your tone would be softer.

How you want the audience to feel:

. . . .
. . . .

7. *If the audience walks away with one thing at all it should be:*

Early on in this section you defined what you want the audience to do at the end and identified the actions that need to take place in order to close. In this objective you are defining the main prerequisite for a successful final close. What I mean is, there is always some fundamental experience, knowledge, perception, belief or feeling that must be in place in order for your audience to want to proceed to the next step. A very simple example would be the issue of trust. Trust is not something that can be achieved by request, as in "Trust me," but rather it is earned through actions and deeds. Throughout this book you have already learned numerous ways to build trust: speak the same language as your audience; show that you are listening; only recommend a solution someone really needs; be passionate; demonstrate your product knowledge; effectively answer questions; keep your commitments. If you do not take steps to build trust, you'll see people hesitating to proceed to the next step, or not proceed at all or cancel your next meeting.

Here's another few examples of things that need to be in place in order to conclude a sale: if you are looking for venture capital, the one thing your audience should walk away with is the belief that the upside opportunity exceeds the downside risk. If you are a small technology company selling leading-edge computer systems to a large organization, you already know that your audience fears that they can't afford to be stuck without support for your systems if your company goes belly up. So if the audience walks away with one thing at all it should be a perception that you are a company with a future.

Once you have defined what your audience needs, create your presentation so your prerequisite for success is firmly entrenched.

In my early years of advertising, going up against the biggest agencies in North America, I knew that if my audience walked away with one thing it would be that my ideas and writing sell, and not just because I was creative, but because I had problem-solving skills. This insight dramatically affected the way I presented my portfolio, which was affectionately referred to as the "bag." While many of my competitors were pitching themselves as creative wonders, I took a different path. Before my audience even saw a sample of my work, the very first thing I did was make a point of presenting the marketing problem my client faced, and then I'd ask my audience how they would tackle such a problem. After they gave it some thought, I would have them turn over the next leaf in my portfolio where they saw the solution. At that point I would mention how my previous client had profited from that very solution. This approach would ensure that it wasn't just my creativity that would become top of mind; it would be my problem-solving ability. That was the real value I brought to the table and why they would pay me more than other freelancers.

For now, give some serious thought as to what dominant feeling, perception or reality needs to be in place in order for your audience to make a commitment. What do you want them to remember most?

If the audience walks away with one thing at all, it should be:

. . . .

. . . .

Basic Ingredients

The next step in the process is to combine what you know of your audience with your stated objectives. When you add them together you end up with a list of all the prerequisites of success that will ensure your objectives are met. These essential elements will determine the content of your presentation and everything else that will make it memorable and effective.

Since these Basic Ingredients are derived from the first two parts of your foundation, you will have to refer back to what you previously listed in both your audience profile and objectives. To make it easier for you to know exactly which areas you need to work with, I have documented your points of reference in a box at the beginning of each section. For your convenience, here is the summary list of all the sections in your audience profile and objectives.

REFERENCE POINT

Define the Audience:

1. The number of people
2. Industry
3. Position
4. Audience expectations
5. The number one issue affecting your audience
6. Audience jargon/buzzwords
7. Audience type

Set Objectives:

1. Length of presentation
2. What you want the audience to do at the end
3. What you want the audience to learn
4. What you want the audience to experience
5. The overall impression you want to impart
6. How you want the audience to feel
7. If the audience walks away with one thing at all it should be:

I have left room at the end of each of the eight main ingredients so you can continue building your upcoming presentation. Got your pen ready? Good. Here we go!

1. Outline the main thoughts you will need to convey.

All you are doing for now is creating a list of the main selling points, benefit statements and anything else that will make your presentation convincing, compelling and informative. This is not your presentation outline. That comes later. This is just a list in point form of all the main thoughts you want to be sure to include in your final presentation. Begin by making sure your main point of discussion is in line with audience expectations or else you will end up disconnecting from your audience rather quickly. It is also a good idea to reference the main issue affecting your audience so you can reach those Greed Glands and command people's attention. Anything you need your audience to learn or experience should be covered, especially since you may need to set up some demonstrations. Last but certainly not least, whatever you think is the most important thing your audience needs to feel, UNDERSTAND or appreciate in order to do business with you, has to be threaded into your main thoughts. So for example, if you need someone to feel comfortable with the idea of making a change of some kind or another, then you need to plant those seeds of persuasion along your field of main thoughts so they will bear fruit in the end.

REFERENCE POINT

Define the Audience:
4. Audience expectations
5. The number one issue affecting your audience

Set Objectives:
3. What you want the audience to learn
4. What you want the audience to experience
7. If the audience walks away with one thing at all it should be:

Main Thoughts:

. . . .

. . . .

. . . .
. . . .
. . . .
. . . .
. . . .
. . . .
. . . .
. . . .
. . . .
. . . .
. . . .
. . . .
. . . .
. . . .
. . . .
. . . .
. . . .
. . . .
. . . .
. . . .
. . . .
. . . .
. . . .
. . . .
. . . .

2. Express yourself with powerful words.

As I have mentioned on several occasions, the words you speak paint images in people's minds, and your audience will move in the direction of those images. So what I need you to do now is find out what the most powerful words in your presentation are. Which ones really resonate with your audience and make a connection? Which ones make the right impression? I'm not suggesting that you need to work through every single word in a presentation. What I am advising is that you be cognizant of the words you speak and that you either identify or create a handful of powerful words that you know will have an impact, and then strategically decide when and how to use them. This will give you greater control over the audience and ultimately over the end result.

Last week I was at a trade show hosted for the food industry. I was there with a friend who worked for a large food distributor who had a booth at the show. I asked my friend's colleague what she wanted to up-sell. "The macaroons," she said. I had tasted them on another occasion and knew that they were amazing. Just then a woman walked up to the display of desserts and I couldn't resist a bit of salesmanship. With a big smile on my face I said to the passer-by, "You have to try the macaroons." She smiled back and asked, "Are they good?" to which I replied, "They're to die for." The woman picked up the macaroon and had a taste. And yes, she loved them.

If you look back at what I said, you will notice how I chose my words carefully to entice the woman to take action. This was my strategy: first of all, I had observed that many exhibitors asked people, "Would you like to try one," and in many cases people politely declined only because they were saving themselves for other samples, since there were hundreds to choose from (how much can you eat?). So instead of asking, I simply told the bystander that she "had to" try one. I also made a point not to say that the macaroons tasted great, but rather that they were "to die for." I chose those words because I not only wanted to leave the impression that these were the best macaroons she would ever experience, but I wanted my audience to actually crave the macaroons. After all, if you just think of having a macaroon you can hold off and resist the calories, but if you have a craving (we've all been there), the resistance level is zero.

Another example comes from the car lot. If you were selling a luxury car, "comfort" is a word with impact. You would describe the ride either as smooth or quiet. These are words that conjure up images that say luxury, and as a bonus, they also make your audience get a feel for that luxury. If I were selling cleaning services, I would want to use the words "shine," or "sparkling." My competition can also make your place clean, but I can make it shine. Just for fun, humor me with this little exercise.

What image comes to mind when you think of your furniture as clean?

. . . .

. . . .

What image comes to mind when you think of your furniture shining?

. . . .

. . . .

The approach that conjures up the most powerful image is the one you should go with. If you were selling a new brand of milkshake, would the words "creamy," or "thick" create an appealing visual for your audience? If you were selling lawn fertilizer you probably would talk about your customers admiring their new, thick green lawns, or better still, talk about how the neighbors would admire your customers' thick green lawns.

Some other powerful words you might use could be ones that reflect the industry jargon or the executive position of your audience because these send a message that you speak the language.

You also want to make sure that the few powerful words you leverage create the right overall impression you want to leave. Do you want to leave the impression that you are an industry expert by using some industry buzzwords or leave an impression that you can communicate to the average consumer by using everyday language? When I speak professionally on my methods, the one word I use more than any other is "control." I do this deliberately, not only because control is the central strategy of my approach, but also because I know that most people's fears or apprehensions dissipate quickly the moment they sense that they are in control. So by using control as a central theme I am gradually making my audience feel more comfortable and receptive to my ideas. In fact, if they walk away with one thing at all, it must be the impression that they are now, for the first time, in control. It's no coincidence that the majority of people I address are motivated to take action after the presentation.

Words have power. They make an impression. Choose yours wisely.

REFERENCE POINT
Define the Audience:
2. Industry
3. Position
5. The number one issue affecting your audience
6. Audience jargon/buzzwords

Set Objectives:
5. The overall impression you want to impart
6. How you want the audience to feel
7. If the audience walks away with one thing at all it should be:

Powerful words:

. . . .
. . . .
. . . .
. . . .
. . . .
. . . .
. . . .
. . . .
. . . .
. . . .
. . . .
. . . .
. . . .

3. Choose the words your audiences WANT TO hear.

You will find that the most powerful words of all are the words that your audiences WANT TO hear. For example, if you are in the transportation industry and you are talking to a manufacturer of fine furniture, that person will probably WANT TO hear the words "scratch-free." This is an issue that's very important. The seniority level of your audience is also a factor in your choice of words. For example, when I am speaking with CEOs and senior VPs I always make a point of using the words "consistency," and "predictability" because those are the prerequisites they need to reach their goals. The interesting thing is how I came across these words. Years ago the former CEO of Bay Networks told me that consistency and predictability were important to him. I figured that they must be important to other CEOs, so I started incorporating them in my presentations, carefully testing the reaction by reading my audience when these words were used. When I noticed that it got them talking and opening up, I kept using them.

You don't have to look very far to find the words your audiences WANT TO hear. In each and every sales call, listen very, very carefully to the words your audiences use in their conversations with you. People are always telegraphing the words they WANT TO hear, but you have to keep your antenna tuned to it.

When you are asking your Control questions (Frame the Pain, What's at Stake), chances are the people you are addressing will tell you words they WANT TO hear. For example, suppose you are a landscape designer. When we first get together you ask me what my impression of a beautiful garden is. "It's full of rich color," I reply. And when you ask me why that's important I tell you, "I need to calm down most of the time because my job is so stressful." When you come back to present your design for my garden you would get my undivided attention by talking about the rich color and how the little waterfall you are building will have a wonderful calming affect. By addressing my expectations (I expect your design to match my definition of a beautiful garden), and speaking my own words back to me, you send the message that you listened and understood what is important to me. You reach through to my Greed Glands. Best of all, since the words are mine, the images they created in my mind make me RELATE to your design and feel truly excited about working with you.

Think back to the last conversation you had with your customers. Whatever words or phrases they frequently refer to are most likely the words that are important to them. As we have said many times before, whatever is important to your audience is important to you.

REFERENCE POINT
Define the Audience:
2. Industry
3. Position
4. Audience expectations
5. The number one issue affecting your audience
6. Audience jargon/buzzwords

Set Objectives:
5. The overall impression you want to impart
6. How you want the audience to feel
7. If the audience walks away with one thing at all it should be:

Words your audiences WANT TO hear:

. . . .
. . . .
. . . .
. . . .
. . . .
. . . .
. . . .
. . . .
. . . .

4. List anything you will need to demonstrate.

When you give a demonstration in your presentation you might be showing someone how a thing works, perhaps bringing a point to life by way of example or enabling someone to experience something. For example, if you were selling lamps you would need to turn them on so the buyer could appreciate what they look like all lit up. If you have something that is complicated to UNDERSTAND, there is nothing quite like a little demonstration to clear things up.

Demonstrations are a visual experience where your audience is shown something. But if you really want to connect with your audience, they should be involved in the demonstration. In other words, get them doing something. There is no experience better than hands-on experience. That experience also makes your presentations more memorable. When I was last looking for a new laptop, the salesperson told me all about the equipment's many features and how easy it was to use. Now between you and me, you can say something is easy to use until the cows come home, but at the end of the day I'll be the judge of that. As for features, I need to see them in action to know if they are of any value. The sales rep must have sensed this because he quickly asked me if I'd like to experience some of the features first-hand. "You bet," I said.

The more someone experiences something first-hand, the more they RELATE to what you are saying.

When you create demonstrations you need to take into account the number of people who are attending. A demonstration for ten people may require a different set-up than one for a single person. For example, if I want to show you some stain-resistant fabrics, it's fairly simple to have you hold a sample and watch as I rub some grease on it so you can see how well the fabric repels stains. But if I was in a trade show and there were fifty people in my audience, I would either need enough samples for everyone to hold, which could prove unfeasible, or take into account that everyone will have to watch the demonstration at the same time. So perhaps I would have a camera capturing the demonstration and project it on a large screen.

You will also need to make allowances for what the audience is expecting to see. If people are expecting to walk away with enough information to make a decision, your demonstration will need to cover more detail than if they were only browsing. You will also need to accommodate the various personality types. Analytical types will want a very methodical demonstration while Type A personalities will want it short, sweet and to the point.

Whether you plan on having one demonstration or a few, you will have to accommodate the overall length of your presentation. That's not to say that you can't have a lengthy demonstration in a short presentation. The demonstration may in fact be the bulk of your presentation, but it would have to be planned that way. Your demonstrations have to finish on time so you don't time-out on your presentation. In my seminars I often try new demonstrations, but it sometimes takes a few presentations to get the timing just right.

If you need your audience to feel comfortable handling a product, then let them try it out. If the overall impression you want to leave is that you are technically proficient, then a demonstration of your abilities might go a long way. If people need to know that what you are offering is a good buy, then a comparison with a competitive product can seal the deal.

Demonstrations:

. . . .

. . . .

. . . .

. . . .

. . . .

REFERENCE POINT
Define the Audience:
1. The number of people
4. Audience expectations
7. Audience type

Set Objectives:
1. Length of presentation
3. What you want the audience to learn
4. What you want the audience to experience
5. The overall impression you want to impart
6. How you want the audience to feel
7. If the audience walks away with one thing at all it should be:

5. Detail important examples / stories.

Examples are a great tool to help your audience UNDER-STAND and RELATE to your message. That's why this book is chock full of them. Examples give clarity and bring your message to life. As you know, people often won't ask questions and so any examples you give are preventative medicine to ensure that they won't need to be asked in the first place. If you find yourself adlibbing an example and it's a hit, make sure to write the example down so you can use it in your next presentation. For example (speak of the devil), if you were an Internet service provider and were talking to me about the reliability of your network, you could really make that point come to life and have some real impact by giving me an example of just how reliable it is; while you're at it, you can also tell me your definition of reliability.

Success stories are also very useful in helping your

audience UNDERSTAND and RELATE, although they need to be used sparingly. If you use them too much you may lose credibility or risk sounding like you are trying to sell too hard. For example, if you are selling a technology that delivers real productivity gains, bring your point to life with a real-life example or case study of how it saved one of your customers a lot of time and the impact it had on that business. If your prospect is a real "people person," they will love to hear how other people were personally affected by your solution. People love success stories for many reasons, the first of which I suppose is because they love to hear about success. Success is uplifting. The fact that success stories demonstrate what is possible is what inspires your audience, and inspiration is powerful in sales. There is also the ancient "herd mentality" where we want what others have, so if someone is benefiting from something, others tend to want it too.

What I find equally fascinating is that people love stories. Period. This love affair with stories starts from the time we are children sitting up in bed listening to imaginative fairy tales and continues to this day when as adults, we take great pleasure in reading a novel. I'm sure Early Man sat around the campfire telling stories, and some went on to express those stories in cave drawings. That would be no coincidence. Stories paint images in our minds and it's our imagination that makes them real. So when you tell a success story, a story of how other customers use your products, or any kind of story to illustrate an example, be sensitive to the fact that you are creating images in the minds of your audience. Are they the right images? Stories make your presentation memorable, and the more memorable your presentation, the easier it will be to move your sales cycle forward.

Just out of interest, your most memorable story is

referred to by professional speakers as your "Signature Story." This is one that people comment on most after your presentation and it's the one they'll talk to others about as well. If you begin to see that you have a Signature Story, you can take your time delivering it because you know the big impact it's going to have on your audience. As we say in show business, milk it for all it's worth.

As you create your stories, make sure to consider the type of people you will be addressing. Type A personalities will prefer shorter stories while others will be fascinated by hearing tales of other people, and still others will want lots of detail. If you are still deciding where a story is needed, consider using one to help your audience learn or experience something you have outlined in your objectives. All stories leave an impression, so it's important to make sure they leave the right impression. For example, if you want people to walk away with the impression that you are well traveled, you could talk about one of your customer experiences overseas, and the more remote the location, the more interesting it might be. When I want to leave the impression that I have worked with most industries, I make sure that each time I give a success story about someone I have coached, I talk about a student from a different industry. One story might be about a financial consultant, another one about someone in the medical profession, and another about the insurance industry, etc. The variety of stories would leave my audience with the impression that I have extensive experience in diverse areas, without me having to spell it out for them.

If you are selling a boat cruise and want your audience to feel the sense of adventure of sailing to faraway places, you could tell a story about one of your excursions to Bali. To really make someone feel they are there, you could describe in your story the incredible flora which is everywhere and the welcoming people of Bali. The more adjectives, the better.

Whatever you do, make sure that the examples and stories that are relevant are planned to achieve an outcome consistent with your objectives.

Throughout this book I've told you countless stories, and all of them were chosen not just to make a point, but to bring each point to life. Do you remember the story about my friend Rod and I and our experience in the hotel in Atlanta? How did you react to it? How did it make you feel? Each time you tell a story, gauge the reaction from your audience. If it only has minimal impact, fix it, discard it or replace it with another. Constantly test the effectiveness of each story until you find and fine-tune the ones that deliver the goods. In no time at all you will be a master storyteller. And that's no fable.

REFERENCE POINT
Define the Audience:
7. Audience type

Set Objectives:
3. What you want the audience to learn
4. What you want the audience to experience
5. The overall impression you want to impart
6. How you want the audience to feel
7. If the audience walks away with one thing at all it should be:

Examples/Success Stories:

. . . .

. . . .

· ·
· ·
· ·
· ·
· ·
· ·
· ·
· ·
· ·
· ·
· ·
· ·
· ·
· ·
· ·
· ·
· ·

6. *Express in simple terms the opportunity you are sharing.*

Sales is all about sharing an opportunity. You need to be able to articulate that opportunity to yourself before you can share it with others; if you can't express an opportunity, how will your audience be able to visualize it and RELATE to it? In fact, when you have a clear image in your mind of the real value you bring to your customers, and you reflect on that before your presentation, you will be more energized and speak more passionately.

Your opportunity is simply an expression of how you can meet your audience's requirements, needs and expectations. Define your opportunity not in terms of what your product is, but rather why someone would buy it. In *How To Make Hot Cold Calls* I refer to this as selling the sizzle. Describe your solutions in terms of the value they deliver because people don't care about your products; they care about finding a solution to a problem or need.

Suppose you were selling a new outdoor paint that would not chip for ten years regardless of weather conditions. This is not about an opportunity for buying paint. How motivating is that? The real opportunity for your customers is in the maintenance-free exterior. The opportunity will vary depending on your audience because what is important to one person or market may not be so to another. If you were selling this paint to home builders they would view this as an opportunity to showcase their commitment to building quality homes and would definitely see the paint as a selling feature worth promoting. They might even have your paint cans on display in their showrooms and give a "before and after" demonstration so customers can experience the difference. If you were selling this paint directly to homeowners, the real opportunity for them could very well be the significant cost savings of only having to repaint once a decade. The opportunity could also be convenience because people won't have to run out and organize the job every few years.

Sizzle makes people WANT TO listen. For example, if I am a banker talking to a small business partnership about a secure line of credit, chances these customers did not wake up in the morning saying, "Hey, today we need a secure line of credit." The people did, however, think about their cash flow crunch. So their Greed Glands will perk up when they hear how they can now secure better cash flow by shaving a few percentage points off their monthly prime rates. The secure line of credit is only a means to that end.

Once you have identified and articulated your opportunity, look for ways for your audience to experience it through examples, demonstrations and stories.

REFERENCE POINT
Define the Audience:
2. Industry
3. Position
5. The number one issue affecting your audience

Set Objectives:
2. What you want the audience to do at the end
4. What you want the audience to experience
6. How you want the audience to feel
7. If the audience walks away with one thing at all it
should be:

The opportunity you are sharing:

. . . .
. . . .
. . . .
. . . .

7. *Detail what is totally unique about your offering/opportunity.*

Now that you have defined your opportunity, let's go the extra mile and make sure that you will have people's undivided attention. Tell them about something they can have right now that has not been available in the past. If you tell me that I can now keep my home exterior looking great for ten years without needing to repaint, and I have not heard of such a wonder product before or couldn't find it anywhere, I'll be all ears. You might be the only person that sells that paint, or the only person who sells it in my area. Either way you will be able to tell me something your competitors can't, which gives your audience one more reason to take action and commit to the next step.

Articulate what is truly unique about your opportunity, your offerings and your company. On the latter point, if you tell people what your company does, you might get them to listen for a minute or two. But if you tell people what makes your company unique, you will pique their interest level and open up a lively discussion. If you don't have anything unique, I urge you to create it. Very often we look for uniqueness in WHAT we offer, but you might also find that you are unique in HOW you offer your products and services. What you offer might be unique only to certain industries or markets, so make sure that whatever you say is unique, is tailored to your audience.

Since your Unique Selling Proposition is so powerful, it would be a good idea to include it as something you want your audience to learn, and it should be memorable enough that they walk away talking about it.

REFERENCE POINT
Define the Audience:
2. Industry
3. Position
5. The number one issue affecting your audience

Set Objectives:
3. What you want the audience to learn
4. What you want the audience to experience
5. The overall impression you want to impart
7. If the audience walks away with one thing at all it should be:

What's unique about your offering/opportunity:

. . . .
. . . .
. . . .
. . . .
. . . .
. . . .
. . . .
. . . .
. . . .
. . . .

8. Main Benefit Statements.

You are giving, you may find yourself presenting the various benefits of your products and services. It is helpful to list them beforehand so you can refer to them easily when needed.

Double check to make sure that your main benefits apply to the industry you are addressing, just in case some benefits are not universal. The same holds true when looking at the seniority level of your audience. If you were in the insurance business you might be selling a type of insurance that has less benefit for senior managers who are already covered by the executive plan.

Take a look to make sure your benefits are in line with your audience's expectations in case they are expecting more value than you can deliver. For obvious reasons the benefits should also address the main issue affecting your audience. If you can communicate your benefits using their jargon and buzzwords, it will help them better RELATE to your message. You might also create two lists of benefits, one short and one longer, to accommodate the needs of the different personality types you are addressing.

REFERENCE POINT
Define the Audience:
2. Industry
3. Position
4. Audience expectations
5. The number one issue affecting your audience
6. Audience jargon/buzzwords
7. Audience type

Set Objectives:
3. What you want the audience to learn
5. The overall impression you want to impart
7. If the audience walks away with one thing at all it
   should be:

Main Benefits:

. . . .
. . . .
. . . .
. . . .
. . . .
. . . .
. . . .
. . . .
. . . .
. . . .

Final Review.

Here's a quick checklist of the eight sections that make up
your Basic Ingredients:

REFERENCE POINT
Basic Ingredients:
1. Main thoughts
2. Powerful words
3. Words your audiences WANT TO hear
4. Demonstrations
5. Examples/Stories
6. The opportunity you are sharing
7. What is totally unique about your offering/opportunity
8. Benefit statements

Once you have completed the important eight steps that define your Basic Ingredients, double check to make sure that all your answers reflect the nature of your audience and that all your answers help you meet your stated objectives.

At this point you have laid the foundation of a successful presentation. You have all the Basic Ingredients to build on, and as you move forward in the process you will constantly refer back to these solid foundation building blocks. These components should not be randomly put together. Everything has to be in its place for a reason, just like any building block you've ever worked with. If you stack blocks two storeys high, you'll never end up with the bungalow you envisioned. So in order to know where all the pieces go and how they fit together, you simply need to create a blueprint that provides the structure for your presentation.

At this point I really need your full attention, so if you have been working non-stop through this process, let's take a break for half an hour and refresh your mind. Get some coffee, take a walk or grab a power nap. Don't do any other work because I want you completely refreshed and ready to create an awesome presentation. If you

already had a break or two and are ready to build, meet me
in the next section.

Outline

Thanks for joining me. If I'd lost my audience now I'd have to call you up and find out where we disconnected so that I wouldn't make the same mistake again. But it looks like you are on board and ready to go. So let's continue. Your outline is made up of the Story and the Script.

The script outline has five components.
- ➡ Script Outline:
  - •Opening Minute
  - •Opening Minute Test
  - •Main Thoughts
  - •Moving Ending
  - •Bridges

Story Outline

A presentation is nothing more than a story of some kind or another. Hopefully it's a compelling story that makes

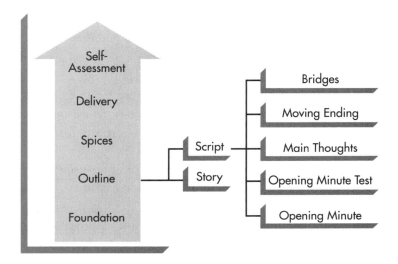

people WANT TO listen and ultimately buy into. You should be able to articulate your story in a single line, which I refer to as your story outline. A story outline is simply the central theme of your presentation.

Yours might be a story about people rejuvenating themselves by taking time to sit in a beautiful, landscaped environment. It might be a story about how busy people can order groceries from their computers at the office and have them on the kitchen table in time for dinner. Your story could be about how people can reach anyone, anywhere, anytime. It may be a story about a transportation company that helps small companies extend their reach into profitable markets they could never before access. It could be stories about helping self-employed people support their families in times of illness. If I were giving a presentation on my favorite ranch in the Rocky Mountains, mine would be a story about a rustic holiday experience where the pressures of the city evaporate in the 12,000 peaks and people are invigorated by the pristine air that is redolent of pine.

Your story outline serves many purposes. First, it tells you what kind of presentation you are building. It also enables you to tell others. In this way it provides a visual road map or thumbnail sketch that you and your audience can use to focus on where you are going. For example, whenever I'm asked about what my presentation on *How To Make Hot Cold Calls* is about, I always reply, "It's about changing people's lives by giving them the power to open new doors of opportunity." Before I give my presentation, which is often in front of large audiences, I always take a moment before going on stage to reflect on those very words, and in doing so I become completely focused on why I'm there, and why my audience is there too. Your story outline also generates ideas because it crystallizes the essence of what you are talking about, and by doing so, your thoughts become more focused.

The litmus test for a good story outline is to answer a most common question: "I heard you are giving a presentation. What's it about?" If you can answer that question effectively you are well on your way.

Your story should address the main issue affecting your audience. If possible it should contain the words your audience WANTS TO hear. It should express the opportunity you are sharing and, if applicable, it should also include what is unique about your opportunity. As you can see, these ingredients all have one thing in common: they speak to your audience's Greed Glands so everyone will WANT TO stay for the presentation.

So what's your story? It's time to put your thoughts into words. Allow me to help you along. Imagine that your presentation is a storybook, and you are going to read that book to your child at bedtime in hopes that it will put your little darling to beddy-byes. (Come to think of it, I suppose this would be the only time you would want to put your audience to sleep!) Your child, filled with anticipation, turns to you and asks, "What's the story about?" What would you tell the little pumpkin that would generate interest and stir the imagination? (If this was a business environment, you would focus on your customer or your customer's customer.)

REFERENCE POINT
Define the Audience:
5. The number one issue affecting your audience

Basic Ingredients:
3. The very words your audiences WANT TO hear
6. The opportunity you are sharing
7. What is totally unique about your offering/ opportunity

This is a story about…

. . . .
. . . .
. . . .
. . . .
. . . .
. . . .
. . . .
. . . .
. . . .
. . . .
. . . .
. . . .
. . . .

Script Outline

Opening Minute

If you are going to grab someone's attention, there is no better time than in the first minute. In fact, if you don't capture someone's attention in the first minute, you might not have an audience around for the rest of the show. Your opening minute sets the direction, tone and atmosphere of your presentation. It has so much influence on your success that I want you to really think this one through. Even if your presentation is informal, or if you are not writing out your presentation in its entirety, your opening minute must be carefully constructed, word for word, and then tested and perfected over time so that even if someone asks you at a barbecue to talk about your company, you can go on autopilot and deliver a knockout opening line. The bottom line on your opening line is that it takes the guesswork out of capturing the attention of your audience.

Don't assume your audience will listen.
Control their desire to listen.

Your opening minute has the power to make people WANT TO listen. The opening minute is like a first impression. It lasts. Since we move in the images we create, your audience will create a set of expectations right in the first minute. Haven't you done that before at the movies? If your audience senses that this is going to be boring or irrelevant, you will have an uphill battle engaging them because they will have turned off or tuned out, or will be headed in that general direction. That goes double for Type A personalities. The opening minute sets the agenda, much like an opening minute would in a business meeting. People will be asking themselves, "Is this important and worth my time?"

There can only be one answer. Absolutely.

Make your opening minute as relevant, compelling and engaging as possible. Let people know that there is great value in having them listen. When I was in university, I majored in ancient history, which was a discipline that taught me the value of stating your case up front. That was what my professors referred to as a thesis, which was preferably one line but could go to two lines if needed. The thesis stated not just the subject matter but also your position on that matter, and then you spent the rest of your essay convincing your reader (line by line) of your position. I transferred that discipline to presentations because people need to know, up front, not just what you are going to talk about and where you are going but why they need to listen. Just as a thesis entices the reader to read on, the opening minute compels your audience to stay tuned as they ask themselves, "How are you going to do that?"

Make sure your opening remarks are in line with audience expectations, and you touch on an issue near and dear to their hearts. Make sure you are speaking their language; if you are speaking about technology to people who are not engineers, don't use technical jargon. If possible, use the very words they WANT TO hear so that they instantly RELATE to your message.

If you want someone to sign up for a membership at the end of your presentation, you could make such a suggestion at the beginning so that you plant the seed from which action will grow. "I'm going to show you how your membership with our company will give you consistent cost savings while increasing the purchasing power of your company." Your opening minute is also an excellent platform to present the opportunity you are sharing.

With only a minute to work with you won't have time to make use of all the reference points that I'm going to give you, but I'm giving them all simply to provide you with enough options and direction. By the same token, the fact that the opening is only a minute long does not diminish its importance. On the contrary: the best Broadway writers have given lots of thought to how shows open and how they close, because the producers of those shows want people glued to their seats right from the start and then up off their seats at the end in a thunderous standing ovation.

Actually, your opening minute does not have to be exactly sixty seconds. This is merely a guideline. If your presentation is only a few minutes, your opening minute might be reduced to opening seconds. For my purpose here, however, I'm presenting the concept in the context of a larger presentation, seminar or speech.

The opening minute is divided into two parts: part one is your opening line, which is your first ten seconds of dialogue. I'm using the term "opening line" to refer more to a single thought rather than a single line. So if your opening thought takes three or four lines within that ten-second window, that's perfectly fine. Part two is the remainder of the opening minute. There is good reason to divide your first minute in this manner. If you were an Olympic speed skater, you would pay special attention to how fast your first few seconds were because that critical beginning can affect your overall timing. A secondary skill is the ability to sustain that speed over the duration of the course.

Here's an example of the two parts in action. Pretend you are talking to customers about your new on-line computer system that makes billing easier. Your opening could go something like this:

Opening line:

"Picture yourself at home, faced with the job of painting your house. You do it because you have to, not because it's enjoyable. Paying your bills is like painting your house."

Rest of opening minute:

"What would you say if I could offer you a tool that would reduce the time it takes to paint your house plus save you some money? Our e-billing works just like this. It will make the task of invoicing much easier. You can view, approve and pay invoices on-line the moment they're created, and it works within your own accounting processes."

Got the hang of it? Take a moment and write out your opening minute. If you don't have a working presentation in front of you just yet, write down the opening minute from your last presentation, whether it was formal or informal.

REFERENCE POINT
Define the Audience:
4. Audience expectations
5. The number one issue affecting your audience
6. Audience jargon/buzzwords
7. Audience type

Set Objectives:
2. What you want the audience to do at the end
7. If the audience walks away with one thing at all it should be:

Basic Ingredients:
3. Words your audiences WANT TO hear
6. The opportunity you are sharing
7. What is totally unique about your offering/ opportunity

Opening Line...

. . . .
. . . .
. . . .
. . . .

Continue with the rest of the opening minute...

. . . .
. . . .
. . . .
. . . .
. . . .
. . . .
. . . .
. . . .

Opening Minute Test

As you know I don't believe in leaving anything to chance. How do you know that your opening minute is going to be as effective as it needs to be? The only way to find out is to test it. After you have completed your opening minute, look at it with a critical eye. Is it compelling enough to get your audience completely focused on what you're saying? What did you say that would make people WANT TO listen to the rest of your presentation? They don't have to. They have legs and comfortable shoes which give them the power to walk out at any time. It's been known to happen. But you want them nailed to their seats. So why do they WANT TO hear more?

Do they UNDERSTAND and RELATE to your opening remarks? If so, they are more likely to listen on. If they don't you will have an instant disconnect from which you may not recover. The last thing you want is to have someone feeling unsure about what you are saying and not asking any questions. They'll be sitting there for the rest of your presentation, stuck on the first minute and still waiting for clarification even though they never expressed their frustration.

I encourage you to use the following scorecard to test the effectiveness of your opening minute. When you use it before your presentation, be sure to specify the exact steps you took to arrive at that score. Simply look at your opening minute and dissect it into various components: those words and phrases which make people WANT TO listen, thoughts that add clarity and images that help people RELATE. If a score is low, take corrective action. For example, if something isn't as clear as it should be, rephrase your thoughts to make your meaning clear. Always think from your audience's perspective. After all, the presentation is for them, not you. I also want you to use this tool after each presentation. Repeat the process I just outlined. The only difference will be that your critique will now be objective because your self-assessment will come from what you observed when you read the audience.

Opening Minute Scorecard
"5" is top score

WANT TO: 1 ☐ 2 ☐ 3 ☐ 4 ☐ 5 ☐

UNDERSTAND: 1 ☐ 2 ☐ 3 ☐ 4 ☐ 5 ☐

RELATE: 1 ☐ 2 ☐ 3 ☐ 4 ☐ 5 ☐

Main Thoughts

With a captivating opening minute well under way, you are ready to work through the main body of your presentation. You can write your main thoughts either in point form or word for word, in other words, writing out your presentation in full. Whichever way you choose, make sure your thoughts are in a logical sequence; any disjointed thought that seems out of place to your audience will put you at high risk of disconnecting. To make sure you stay connected, incorporate the information you carefully earmarked in your Basic Ingredients. All the raw material you need to reach your objectives is already there. That's why the Basic Ingredients is your main source for content. If your presentation is divided into various parts, start by outlining the sections and then under each one make a list of your various thoughts, points or subject matter. When you have completed this exercise you will want to come back and weave in your Bridges and Spices, which you will learn about further on in the process.

REFERENCE POINT
Basic Ingredients:
1. Main thoughts
2. Powerful words
3. Words your audiences WANT TO hear
4. Demonstrations
5. Examples/Stories
6. The opportunity you are sharing
7. What is totally unique about your offering/ opportunity
8. Benefit statements

In sequential order, detail the main thoughts of your presentation:

- . . . .
- . . . .
- . . . .
- . . . .
- . . . .
- . . . .
- . . . .
- . . . .
- . . . .
- . . . .
- . . . .
- . . . .

Moving Ending

Endings need to end on an up note. They should be memorable (remember *Gone with the Wind*?). Since it's the last thing people see or hear, your ending will be one of the first things your audience remembers. Like your opening minute, the ending has to be written word for word and then tested and perfected over time. You never want a good ending. You want a *knockout* ending! There are several techniques for creating your powerful ending. The first is, try to tie your ending back to your opening so that you can bring your presentation full circle. It forces people to recap your whole presentation in a matter of just seconds.

Allow me to use one of my presentations as a simple example. Here's one of my opening lines:

"I'd like you to think of one career-making opportunity you'd love to participate in. Take a moment and write it down. (I wait about fifteen seconds while they do.) Your ability to make that happen is what we're going to talk about today. Your success at opening that door of opportunity comes down to effectively communicating your unique value in less than thirty seconds."

I have my audience completely focused on their next big opportunity and they are listening to find out how to make it happen. After I review my system for an hour or more, I come back to where we all started. Here are my closing remarks that tie it all together:

"Remember the opportunity you wrote down at the very beginning?
You have the power to take control and make it happen."

The second technique has to do with using the words of your audience, because there is nothing they RELATE to more. At the beginning of your initial sales call your customer told you about the challenges they were facing and what's at stake. Imagine that you are a banker and when you ask me what I feel could be improved with my finances, I answer, "I wish I could get better organized and keep track of where all my investments are." When you ask what happens when I can't keep track of my investments, I reply, "I'm always missing opportunities that I could have profited from." As you come to the end of your three-minute presentation on your banking services, you could use my very words by saying something like "…and that's how it's now possible for you to be better organized with your finances and never lose sight of a good investment opportunity."

As a third option, tie your ending into the one thing

you want the audience to walk away with. For example, if you want them to walk away with a sense that you have the resources to get the job done, make sure you mention that in closing. If you want your audience to commit to a medical examination, you could reference that by saying something like, "…all those benefits begin with a simple medical exam that is done at your convenience" or, "…after a successful medical exam you can be covered for disability and then get on building your business with confidence."

The ending is divided into two parts: closing thoughts and the closing line. The closing thoughts can last a minute or two which build to the climax, or in other words, the closing line. Make sure you choose your words carefully because this is when you want the big impact. You will also want to say your closing line slowly to ensure that your audience has the time to hear, digest and relish every word.

REFERENCE POINT
Script Outline:
Opening Minute

Taking the Reins:
Frame the Pain
What's at Stake

Set Objectives:
7. If the audience walks away with one thing at all it should be:

Closing thoughts...

. . . .
. . . .
. . . .
. . . .
. . . .

Closing line...

. . . .
. . . .
. . . .
. . . .

Bridges

Unless your presentation is only a minute long, it most likely consists of a series of different thoughts carefully joined together. In order for your audience to follow your train of thought, each section or subject has to be presented in a logical sequence.

For example, when I am giving a seminar on *How To Make Hot Cold Calls,* my first three sections deal with Reach (the ability to get people on the phone), and then Convincing Words (the scripting process), and then Speaking Passionately (the way you deliver those words). Since I'm going to be jumping from one train of thought to another, there has to be a logic flow in order for the audience to follow me and make sense of it all. I have to let the audience know what the relationship is between one section and another.

Here's how my thoughts connected:

Reach: When you apply all those techniques, you will be able to get all your decision makers on the phone.

Convincing Words: Now that you have your prospect on the phone, what are you going to say?

Speaking Passionately: Twice as important as what you say is how you say it.

Notice the logic flow is obvious. After talking about how to reach people, it makes sense to talk about what you are going to say to them, and after talking about what to say to them it makes sense to talk about how you deliver those words.

What you see by this example is that each segue from one main thought to another is a bridge of connecting thought. Like a series of bridges on the highway, it keeps you and your passenger going to the end destination without getting lost. You need to ask yourself, "Is there a reason why I'm going on to the next section? What does one thought have in common with the one preceding it and the one after it? Why does the participant need to listen further?" The bridges you build keep your audience connected to your thoughts.

Thoughts connect. People connect to thoughts.

If there is no flow of logic to your thoughts, your audience will disconnect. Worse, they may never tell you. You might just be lucky enough to catch it in time when you read the audience and see that glassy-eyed look. Have you ever been in a presentation where you caught yourself asking, "What are they talking about? Why is he saying that?" Those were times when you disconnected because there was no logic flow from one area to another. When you have strong, clear connecting thoughts you create an environment that enhances your audience's level of understanding.

These bridges of logic also give you an amazing opportunity to read the audience to make sure they are with you. You can do this by simply posing your bridge in the form of a question. As you recall, that's exactly what I did in the first segue in my presentation for Convincing Words where I asked the audience, "Now that you have your prospect on the phone, what are you going to say?" I pause after that to see their reaction, whether they answer the question directly or lean forward in anticipation.

Bridges also serve one other very important function. They provide your audience with a road map that helps them stay focused. If they're focused, they're connected. For example, suppose I was talking to you about estate planning. In my conversation I covered financial planning, tax planning and wills. What does financial planning have in common with tax planning? Answer: two sides of the same coin. So after my talk on financial planning I could segue into tax planning with a line like:

"But always remember, what you're left with is just as important as what you make."

At that point you'd be thinking "Steve's got a point there" and your next thought might even be, "Those damn taxes!" Now you definitely WANT TO hear what I'm going to say next. Just as important, you UNDERSTAND what I'm talking about and where I'm going. Better still, you can RELATE to what I'm talking about. The result: I have your undivided attention, at least for now, and I can proceed to talk about tax planning in the knowledge that you are listening.

After my riveting discussion on tax planning (cut me some slack there…), I need a logical reason to go into the next topic of discussion, which is wills. I'm sure there are dozens of links here, but for the sake of example let's use the following:

"Now that you've gone to great lengths to secure all your accumulated wealth, make sure that the people you want to leave it to actually get it."

You are thinking, "I'm not leaving it to the government!" Now the coast is clear to talk about wills. By the way, since some people in my audience might already have a will, I know I will need a pre-emptive statement to keep them connected. (If they already have a will, they may not RELATE to my message.) So I just might embellish my segue a little:

"Now that you've gone to great lengths to secure all your accumulated wealth, make sure that the people you want to leave it to actually get it. That's why wills are important. Even if you have a will as we speak, over time things change either with your finances or the people in your life, which is why you always need to review your will from time to time. Even if you find no changes, you might need to consider holding your assets in trust so they cannot be touched in a lawsuit."

Just as bridges provide your audience with a road map, you can use the same road map to remember where you are going in case your mind ever goes blank. For example, suppose you have six bridges in your presentation and your mind goes blank somewhere after the third bridge. To get yourself back on track, all you would have to do is remember where your last bridge was, and you will instantly know which direction your presentation is supposed to take, which in this example would be bridge number four.

There are three main places to build your bridges: one between the opening minute and the main body, several within the main body, and one between the main body and your ending. When you are looking at the bridges within the main body, watch for either distinct breaks in subject matter or thoughts.

Bridge between Opening Minute and Main Body...

. . . .
. . . .

Bridges within Main Body...

. . . .
. . . .
. . . .
. . . .

Bridge between Main body and Ending...

. . . .
. . . .

When you have completed your bridges, insert them back into the main body you previously compiled. As you put all the connecting thoughts into their correct places (like filling in pieces of a puzzle), you will begin to fill in the gaps and see your presentation start to take shape in a more formal sense. Since the bridges have a logic flow, you will now be able to stand back and check to see that your main body follows the same logical sequence. It is quite possible that you will find some of the content you outlined in your main body out of order. Should that be the case, you will need to adjust some of your sections to reflect the proper flow of your presentation.

Spices

By now your story outline should already contain elements that make your presentation engaging, exciting and memorable. But now it's time to take that extra step and spice it up a little, or a lot depending on taste. At the beginning of this Presentation section I mentioned that planning a presentation is like planning a dinner party based on what you know about your audience. I said that one of the things you need to know is how to spice your food depending on your audience's tastes. Well, just as spices can make or break a great meal, you can spice up your presentation in all sorts of ways, again within range of what is acceptable to the type of audience you are addressing.

Whether you are naturally gifted at presenting, a large part of your ability to deliver an outstanding presentation comes from the use of certain time-honored theatrical devices that are very well planned. I call these devices the Spices.

Spices add variety and an additional layer of clarity. Spices turn the ordinary into the extraordinary. Spices make things interesting. The more interesting your presentation, the more your audience will be captivated.

I have to admit that of all the art that goes into making a great presentation, none gives me more satisfaction and greater joy than the Spices. I have been looking forward to writing this section ever since the idea of this book first came to mind. Spices have the most dramatic impact on your presentation, and in some cases will exceed the wildest expectations. I mean that. Let's open up the spice rack and see what we have:

- Examples
- Demonstrations
- Magic Moment
- Visual Snapshot
- Props

- Stories
- Participation Points
- WOW!
- Visuals

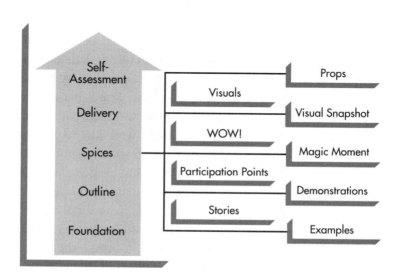

Yummmmm. A performer's use of these nine Spices is called showmanship. Spices are about connecting with your audience by stimulating their minds and senses. It's about engaging your audience so they feel a part of your presentation and not apart from it. When I taste a truly great dish my first response is to ask the chef, "What spices did you put in this?" What have *you* put in *yours*?

Bring your presentation to life by adding the spice of life.

So now let's take a look at presentation Spices. By the way, my apologies if all this talk about food is making you hungry. If you need to excuse yourself to get a snack, I'll UNDERSTAND. Just put a bookmark here so you'll know where you left off. I'll continue anyway for those readers who can hold off until dinner. The rest of you will catch up when you get back from the fridge.

Bring on the Spices!

Examples

How do you spice up an example, you ask? Good question. Let's find out how to turn an ordinary example into an extraordinary example. Suppose you are selling a computer application and want to discuss its productivity gains. You might very well decide that, for the sake of credibility, it is essential to give a real-life example of the productivity gains that one of your other customers actually achieved by using your application. You can drive the point home by referencing exact numbers. The more specific you can be with facts and figures, the more interesting your example becomes, and you get people saying things like, "I didn't know that!" You also get people asking questions. That's all goodness as far as you're concerned.

Don't take your hand away from the spice rack just yet.

What would you say to the idea of bringing those figures to life by telling a story about how those gains affected one of your customer's businesses? It's worth a shot.

Not spicy enough for you? How about personalizing the story by giving an example of the kinds of gains that your audience can expect to see in their own organization? Why just talk about another customer's experience when you can also bring the point closer to home? That would go a long way to making your audience better RELATE to your presentation. It will also increase Greed Gland activity. But hold on, we're not done yet. You can get your audience to participate in the example by asking them a question, such as, "What would productivity gains like that mean to your company?" or, "Have you seen gains like that before?" Questions get an audience involved, and when they are involved, they are connected.

Wait a minute. Not spicy enough for you? OK. You want spice. You'll get spice. Combine your example with a little demonstration. Take out a calculator for visual effect and calculate those productivity gains. Better yet, add more spice by placing the calculator in the hands of your audience and have them do the calculation. That way they are participating in the example, and they can actually see the figures appear in front of their very own eyes. That kind of immediate visual impact imprints the figures directly into the mind, which creates an emotional response (WOW!), adds credibility (they did the calculation and saw the numbers for themselves), and makes both the experience and the figures memorable. By now you probably have observed an interesting overlap of Spices:

Example ➜ *Demonstration* ➜ *Prop* ➜ *Audience participation*

An example can lead to a demonstration, which can

lead to the use of a prop, and greater audience participation. This overlap happens naturally and is absolutely encouraged. The more these various elements are included and working synergistically, the greater will be your ability to command attention.

One of the most effective ways to spice up your examples is to use metaphors and similes. There are several of them throughout this book. Do you recall the advice my Uncle Butch gave me? This was a simile. I'll repeat it here so you can see what I mean:

> "Steven, building a business is like building a house.
> If you want to build a house to live in, you have to
> have a strong foundation."

By using a simile my Uncle Butch made his point clear. He made me UNDERSTAND very quickly. His simile also implanted a strong visual in my mind, which was easy to remember. In fact, the use of similes and metaphors is one of the most effective ways to get your audience to RELATE to what you are saying. This morning I met with Marnie Styles, a dedicated and very successful Financial Planner at RBC Investments. She was reviewing a presentation on telephone prospecting that she was giving to her peers at a conference.

Marnie began her presentation by telling the audience that when you make a telephone sales call, you are doing what prospectors did in the gold rush days of the Klondike, and that is, panning for gold. She then went on to ask different members of the audience which tools the prospectors used. The answers included pickaxes, mules, gold pans etc. Then Marnie asked about the processes people used to pan for gold. The audience talked about how the prospectors had to walk through riverbeds to pan for the gold, sifting through silt and mud until the nuggets appeared for the lucky few. Marnie proceeded to say that, in the twenty-first century, the prospecting tool is the telephone. She then had everyone take out their cell phones and hold them up. "There's gold on the other end," she continued. Marnie completed her introduction by saying, "That's the tool. What's the process? That's what we're going to be talking about."

Notice how the metaphor was used as an example, which was then turned into a prop, which resulted in more audience participation. By having people hold up their cell phones it showed them that their opportunities were close at hand and very real. They could actually feel it. Marnie reinforced this idea by ending the seminar holding up her cell phone and saying, "There is gold in the palm of your hands."

Now what about your similes and metaphors? You can literally create one for every concept, product or service incorporated in your presentations. Here's a simple process for creating your awesome metaphors:

Subject matter:

. . . .
. . . .

Ask yourself, "What is it like?"

. . . .
. . . .
. . . .

How so?

. . . .
. . . .
. . . .

To use Uncle Butch's simile again, the subject is building a business. What's building a business like? Building a
business is like building a house. How is building a business like building a house? If you want to build a house,
you have to have a strong foundation.

I think you get the hang of what we're trying to do
here. Experiment with different examples to see which
simile and metaphor works best. That's all part of the fun.
You might even embellish an example when you adlib.
When you find you have a winner, you can use it again in
your next presentation.

Before I continue, I want to make sure that you have an
opportunity to master this skill. So here's a little exercise
I'd like you to do. Either take one of your examples you
listed in the Basic Ingredients section or create a new one.
Now find creative ways to make that example more interesting. I'll give you a road map to navigate your thoughts
and get your creative juices going.

Example:

. . . .

. . . .

What you want your example to accomplish:

❑ *Help your audience UNDERSTAND*
❑ *Help your audience RELATE*

What can you add to your example to make a point easier to UNDERSTAND?

Areas that need clarity:

. . . .

. . . .

Words, descriptions, thoughts, facts or figures that will add clarity:

. . . .
. . . .
. . . .
. . . .

What part of your example do you think your audience can RELATE to? (Do they RELATE from personal or business experience?)

. . . .
. . . .

How can you modify your example so that it takes place in your customer's own environment?

. . . .
. . . .

How can your audience participate in the example?

. . . .
. . . .

What similes/metaphors come to mind?

. . . .
. . . .

Final example (in full or point form):

. . . .
. . . .

Once you have carefully created an example, the next consideration is a crucial one. You need to move from "What" to "Where." In other words, now that you know what your example is, you have to plan where you want it placed. The positioning of your Spices is a strategic decision that requires thought, patience, and trial and error to get it just right. It's a lot like interior decorating. Just as important as the furniture you buy is where you place it. If your television is in the room, you will want to position your couch so that everyone can watch the programs. If there is no television in the room, your couch can go anywhere, as long as it does not get in anyone's way. But even then you have to decide which wall it goes against, which window you want to sit under, or you may need to consider how the couch interacts with the two loveseats.

If you are offering an example to clarify a point, your choice of where your example goes is limited because it will have to follow the point you just made. If your examples are more general, you have greater flexibility as to where you put them. My only point is that placement is not arbitrary. You also want to watch to make sure you don't have too many examples lumped together because you might run the risk of confusing people with too much to comprehend and remember. Make sure to spread examples out to keep your presentation interesting at all times.

One way to know if you need to either add an example, or move an existing example to another spot in your presentation, is by tuning into the questions that are being asked. Have you ever been asked to clarify a point only to say to your audience, "I was getting to that in a few minutes." Well, your audience has just informed you that your example appears a few minutes too late. The next time you give the same presentation move the example so people won't have to ask the question again. Remember what we talked about earlier: people may not tell you that they don't UNDERSTAND and you can lose your audience without knowing what happened. Read your audience and adjust your examples accordingly.

Here's a simple grid to help you plan your examples. You will be using the same kind of grid for all your Spices.

Example   Positioning

. . . .
. . . .

Example   Positioning

. . . .
. . . .

Example   Positioning

. . . .
. . . .

The last point I want to make on the subject of examples has to do with your delivery. (This part is really interesting, so pay close attention.) Using our previous example about calculating productivity gains, what would happen if you just pulled out a calculator and said, "Steven, let's take a minute and figure out the exact productivity gains your company can realize?"

Hold it right there.

Regardless of how I answer, what assumption did you make? No, I'm not going to tell you right away. Give it some thought.

Underlying assumption:

. . . .
. . . .

Since you asked me a question you were assuming I

was listening. But what if I wasn't? What if my mind was stuck on something you said five minutes ago? Do you remember when we were talking about how to offer the solution, and I recommended that you ask permission first by prefacing your solution with the phrase, "May I share it with you?" The same holds true here. For example, you could say something like, "Steven, I think it would be helpful if you could see the actual productivity gains for your own team. I have a simple method of figuring it out. Would you like to help me with the calculation?" If people say yes you have their undivided attention, and if they say no you have an opportunity to address whatever they need. You might be speaking with someone who does not need the calculation in order to make a decision, and you would only be frustrating the individual if you were to proceed. In any event, this gives you one more moment to read the audience to make sure you are, in fact connected. If you have lots of examples you should only apply this technique with a few of them. You don't want to come across as someone who is unsure of yourself, which I know is not the case here. If it were me, I would ask permission for the first example and then again for one close to the end just so I know my audience has stayed with me in between. Choosing when to ask permission should be planned and tested, just like how you decide where to use your examples.

Stories

If you want to spice up a success story or you have a story to tell about the experience of one of your other customers, there are simple ways to turn a good story into a great story. I suppose I should be asking you what makes a good story and a great story. Here's my take on it: a good story informs and a great story inspires. When you listen to a good story you can picture the characters. When you listen to a great story you feel as though you know the characters. An audience listens to a good story. A great story draws them right into the story.

A story by its very nature is an extremely visual device, and the more interesting the visuals you paint in people's minds, the more memorable your story becomes. Look for opportunities to add descriptive words that will make the images of your story more visual. That's what adjectives and adverbs are for. Here's a brief story I've quickly put together in two versions. It's a story told by a gardener who is talking to a prospective customer about his lawn care service. The gardener is turning a customer testimonial into a story to promote his excellent service. You tell me which one is more visual and why.

Gardener talking to prospect (Version 1):

There's a customer of mine who lives near you in a brick house and she keeps her lawn in good shape. She travels a lot on business like you and she told me that one of the nicest things I ever did for her was to water her lawn one day when she was away. You remember that week last summer when we had that record heat wave? Well, I noticed her lawn was turning brown in some spots so I watered it while I worked on the rest of the homes on her street. It wasn't a big deal, but the way I look at it, your lawn has my name on it and my reputation is everything to me.

Gardener talking to prospect (Version 2):

There's a retired customer of mine who lives two streets from you in a beautiful two-storey gold brick house on a cul-de-sac and she keeps her lawn in immaculate shape. She travels a lot and she told me that one of the nicest things I ever did for her was water her lawn one day when she was away. You remember that week last summer when we had that record heat wave and it was so hot even the mosquitoes were ducking for shade? Well, I noticed her grass was slowly turning brown in some spots around the middle of the lawn so I gave it a good soaking while I worked on the rest of the homes on her street. It wasn't a big deal, but the way I look at it, your lawn has my name on it and my reputation is everything to me.

Which story is more interesting? (Hopefully you answered story number two). The second story simply gives the audience a more graphic picture and, as a result, people create more images in their minds that help them RELATE to it better.

Before I spill the beans and show you which words create the stronger visuals, take a moment and circle the words or phrases in the second version that bring the story to life. While you are doing that I'll grab another cup of coffee…

How did you make out? Let's take a quick review of some of the changes that made the story more appealing. What I'll do is outline each enhancement and follow it with a brief explanation on how it affects the audience.

"retired"

Qualifying the type of customer is important especially because it helps the audience immediately RELATE to the story, especially if audience members are also retired. People in the audience might say to themselves, "That person is just like me. She probably spends half her day in her garden now that she has lots of time on her hands." With just one word the gardener captures attention.

"two streets from you"

If the gardener had simply said that his customer lived in a brick house in the neighborhood, you wouldn't have given that comment a second thought if all the homes in your neighborhood were brick. But by making you picture only those homes two streets away, the image in your mind became more focused, and therefore more meaning-ful. If you happened to know people two streets away you would RELATE to that image all the more.

"beautiful two-storey gold"

It wasn't just a brick house, it was a beautiful brick house which makes one think that someone owning a beautiful house probably pays a lot of attention to main-taining a beautiful garden. Adding that it was a two-storey house makes listeners focus that much harder on the story because in a nanosecond they use their imagination to draw a two-storey picture in their minds. The use of color is also powerful because color is very specific. It wasn't a red brick home; the bricks were gold. The image of a gold brick home adds to the total image of the home that has been portrayed so far (it's beautiful, has two floors with gold bricks), making the total image more dra-matic and complete.

"on a cul-de-sac"

What do you picture when you think of a cul-de-sac? For me, the first thing that comes to mind is the image of a semi-circular street followed by an image of children playing football or hockey on the road because there is no traffic to worry about. What comes to mind for you? It's a very visual phrase and, like I said, the more dynamic the images, the more engaged the audience becomes.

"immaculate"

Now if you love gardening as much as I do, take a second and write down (don't spare the words) what comes to mind when you think of an immaculate garden.

Images of an immaculate garden:

. . . .
. . . .
. . . .

Now imagine the impact of all those impressions in your mind in the space of a split second. Imagine the emotions. I would think that the more passionate one is toward one's garden, the more graphic these images would be and the more potent their effect on the audience.

"and it was so hot even the mosquitoes were ducking for shade"

Now that's a heat wave! A phrase like that makes you feel the heat, and if you are feeling the heat you are not outside the story—you are in it. It also makes you picture mosquitoes, and I swear you can even hear them heading toward you. Bzzzzzzzzzzzzzzzzzzz. What comes to mind when you think about mosquitoes ducking for cover?

"slowly"

"Slowly" is one of those words you can say slowly to deliver the most impact. At this point, the listener is not just picturing the poor woman's immaculate lawn turning brown, but the devastation that is creeping up hour by searing hour.

"around the middle of the lawn"

By being specific about exactly where the lawn is turning brown, the gardener knows exactly what his audience is thinking at that precise moment: you are focused on the middle of the lawn. This effect is the epitome of controlling your audience's thoughts.

"gave it a good soaking"

Talk about dedication. This gardener didn't just water his customer's lawn, he gave it a good soaking! This phrase conjures up lots of water, sprinkler going back and forth, for hours and hours and hours. You can feel how wet that lawn is. And what's that you see? A puddle in the middle of the lawn? Is that lawn starting to look green?

As you have noticed by now, I am often giving you my interpretation of the kinds of images each of these words and phrases conjure up. But you have your own images. That's the interesting part of the exercise. No two people in the audience will see the same visuals. That's not just a function of their imagination. It's how they RELATE to your story. A business owner can RELATE to other business owners or the issues other business owners face every day. So if you are talking to a business owner and you are telling a story about an experience one of your customers had, your story will be more meaningful to your audience if the customer in your story is also a business owner.

So what's your story? Have you given any thought to using stories to spice up your presentation? To help you create a story, here's a brief process to help you kick-start some ideas.

What is the objective of your story? What do you want it to accomplish?

. . . .

. . . .
. . . .
. . . .

What kinds of details will the audience need to learn
so you can achieve your objectives?

. . . .
. . . .
. . . .
. . . .

List all the elements in your story (people, places,
things, situations etc.).

. . . .
. . . .
. . . .
. . . .

Identify only those elements your audience can
RELATE to.

. . . .
. . . .
. . . .
. . . .
. . . .

Try adding descriptive words to introduce the people
and places in your story.

. . . .
. . . .
. . . .
. . . .
. . . .

What do you want people to remember most about your story?

. . . .
. . . .
. . . .
. . . .

What would make your story more memorable?

. . . .
. . . .
. . . .
. . . .

Does it have a catchy ending?

. . . .
. . . .
. . . .
. . . .

Final story:

. . . .
. . . .
. . . .
. . . .
. . . .
. . . .
. . . .
. . . .
. . . .
. . . .
. . . .
. . . .
. . . .
. . . .

Did you achieve your objectives? If not, what needs to be added, removed or enhanced?

. . . .
. . . .
. . . .
. . . .
. . . .

Don't forget to make sure you know where each story will be positioned in your presentation—and why these stories go where they go.

Story   Positioning

. . . .
. . . .

Story   Positioning

. . . .
. . . .

Story   Positioning

. . . .
. . . .

Demonstrations

Demonstrations add a different kind of experience to the presentation. Suppose you are my interior designer and one day you drop by my home to show me a couple of really interesting lamps that you know I need. You probably would have noted under Basic Ingredients that you needed to bring them along to show me how they match my existing decor. Seeing is believing, *n'est-ce pas*? At any rate, in advance of coming over you would have done your homework and given some serious thought as to how you would present the lamps. You can just plunk them down on the end tables and show me how they pick up on the other elements in the room. You can spice up your presentation by demonstrating how these lamps create a different mood with the light they throw; you can have me turn off all the lights and then turn on the lamps one at a time, stopping to comment on what I observe each time new light is introduced to the room. Actually, if you do that you will also give me an opportunity to experience the kinds of shadows thrown. Shadows add texture, and texture adds another dimension of interest to your presentation.

Notice how your demonstration was most interesting when you had me actively participate. The more your audience gets directly involved, the more memorable the experience becomes. When people simply watch a demonstration, they are not a part of it. When they participate, it becomes their demonstration, not yours, and because of that they RELATE to it on a deeper level, and connect with you. Also keep in mind that people learn in different ways: watching, listening, speaking, doing, reading, writing, drawing, touching, tasting. Demonstrations help your presentation by touching on many of these learning modes.

I'm a very tactile kind of guy. You can describe the material of a suit jacket to me all you want, but I always end up having to touch the fabric to feel the texture. I'm sure that when you go out for dinner the smell of the food and the presentation is just as important to you as the taste. Why do you think some restaurants display their desserts on a portable dessert cart? Not only can you see how great the desserts look, and by association how wonderful they taste, but the waiters can also weaken your resolve just by casually strolling down the aisle a couple of times pushing the dessert cart.

So when planning your demonstrations, spice them up by creating ways to get people involved and using their senses. If the purpose of your demonstration is to have people learn something, tell your audience what you want them to learn, explain why, do your demonstration and then have your audience try. Then ask them how it was helpful. If you are demonstrating something to clarify a point, concept or idea, spice it up with props (we'll be talking more about props in a few minutes).

Got your pen handy? Let's add a demonstration to the presentation you're currently building. There is no time like the present.

What do you want to demonstrate?

. . . .
. . . .
. . . .
. . . .

What is the objective of the demonstration?

. . . .
. . . .
. . . .
. . . .

What is your audience expecting to see in a demonstration?

. . . .
. . . .
. . . .
. . . .

How can you get your audience participating?

. . . .
. . . .
. . . .
. . . .

Specifically what will you be doing, and what will your audience be doing?

. . . .
. . . .
. . . .
. . . .

If you have a large audience, how can everyone participate?

. . . .
. . . .
. . . .
. . . .

I find it helpful to have several versions of any given demonstration. If I know that my audience is full of Type A personalities, then I will have a shorter version or one that is faster paced. If I know that I have analytical types, then I keep extra documentation on hand for after the demonstration. Regardless, I always anticipate questions so I can answer them effectively or perhaps answer them before they even need to be asked.

Once each of your demonstrations has been determined, it is time to give some thought as to where they should be placed. Timing, as you know by now, is everything. If a demonstration appears too early or too late it loses its effectiveness and alienates the audience. When I was out last night shopping for a new cell phone, the sales rep noticed that I was spending some time studying two different models. He knew I was interested by the fact that I asked a lot of questions, trying to discern the difference in value between the two. He picked up the phones and began demonstrating some of the features for me so I could see first-hand what each phone could deliver. (Demonstrating the features was more effective than just explaining the features.) If this fellow had shown me the features before I had shown enough interest in a particular model, he would have turned me off because I wasn't ready to see them just yet.

Demonstration   Positioning

. . . .
. . . .

Demonstration   Positioning

. . . .
. . . .

Demonstration   Positioning

. . . .
. . . .

Participation Points

On several occasions we have looked at the importance of having your audience participate in your examples and demonstrations. Participation is a fundamental theatrical device used by the best performers the world over. Participation makes people RELATE to your presentation on a more personal level. In some way, I suppose participation is a form of commitment because your audience is agreeing to do something with you. Voluntary participation also fosters a WANT TO frame of mind. In fact, participation is the DNA found in all great presentations.

A presentation is a two-way conversation and not a one-way performance.

Unfortunately, the word "present" brings to mind someone standing alone and doing all the talking. The best presenters know differently. You build a strong connection with your audience by engaging them.

When your audience participates in your examples and demonstrations or any other part of your presentation, they are actually helping you build your presentation. As a result, they are more likely to WANT TO listen and move the conversation forward. This is because people support that which they help create. Participation also brings you and the audience closer together. Through hands-on involvement you move away from a situation where it is, "Them and You" and move instead toward a state of "Us."

You might find that some of your best adlibs come from the moments when your audience is involved in the presentation. They too can come up with amazing comments and one-liners and even suggestions on how to improve something they are working on with you. For example, you might be demonstrating the features of a new product and in the process of helping you demonstrate, an audience participant discovers a whole new application for it or a better way of explaining a feature. The person might ask questions outside the ones you had anticipated and add more substance to your presentation. Each time people participate they bring their own style and personality to the presentation, which often brings a whole new set of ideas to the table.

Audience participation can be as subtle or dynamic as you want. When I give my speeches, I often start by greeting participants as they come in the door, shaking their hands and thanking them for coming. I do this not just because people love to be welcomed, but because it engages them in the presentation even before it begins. All I've done is close the gap between them and me, between audience and speaker. The physical connection of the handshake instantly makes a personal connection. It establishes a relationship. It feeds and creates energy. Getting people involved gives me an opportunity to hear people's voices and get a glimmer of insight into their personalities, which helps me read the audience later on. It even helps me zero in on their expectations. From a motivational point of view, this technique enables me to focus on the whole audience as if on a one-on-one basis.

Participation might comprise something as simple as asking a question or opening up the conversation to hear different viewpoints. For example, suppose you were giving a presentation to some prospective customers, and the topic was how your company has been rated by consumer groups. You could begin by handing each participant a sheet of paper containing a list of all the areas your company was rated on, like responsiveness, innovation, service, customer satisfaction etc. At the bottom is a line that says "Other," in case there is another area people feel should be assessed. (This encourages more participation.) You would then invite participants to score the items according to what they feel is important in a company. For example, they might rate service first, innovation second etc. When they finish you would review how they prioritized the list to see how opinions differed. You would then compare how the consumer groups rated your company. Let's look at what this simple form of audience participation achieved: the sheet with the list acted as a prop that got people to take an active role in your presentation. It also enabled you to read the audience because it told you what's important to them. It also made your audience WANT TO listen to what you said next because they were curious as to how your company performed in the areas that they identified as important. As well, the participation shifted the focus of your presentation—it became focused on audience issues.

You can also increase participation by setting time aside for a question-and-answer session. To do this well, make sure you create an environment where people feel comfortable asking questions and contributing answers. Little things help, like saying, "That's an excellent question!" If you welcome questions it will show in the smile on your face and the passion with which you answer.

You can increase the level of participation by making questions challenging, with the result that your audience has to think harder for the answer. You can also try changing the nature of your questions. For example, suppose in your presentations you regularly hand out a map of North America and ask your prospects to identify where their products are sold today, and where they would like to sell them in the near future. You can open up a whole different dialogue by changing the question. Why not try asking them to identify markets where they could maximize their revenue?

Participation might include something as basic as having someone write something on the board, working out some figures on a calculator, or visiting a Web site. If you were walking someone through a catalogue, why not have the person turn the page? How about handing someone a pair of scissors (another interesting prop) and asking that person to cut out items of interest? How about having someone hand you something? There is no limit to the ways you can get people involved. It doesn't matter if you are addressing one person or a thousand, just get them doing something.

When I used to perform magic I discovered early on how I could WOW! an audience by elevating audience participation. Instead of doing the card trick in my hands, it was ten times more powerful when I put the deck in other's hands, instructed them on what to do, and let the trick unfold as if they were doing it themselves.

For obvious reasons, you don't want people participating in every minute of your presentation. Pick your moments carefully. Either you need someone to do something because it is essential for that person to learn (when they are participating in a demonstration or example of some kind), or the participation is simply added to boost the energy level in the room and increase the fun. As you have seen with the other Spices, positioning is crucial. Don't lump all your participation in one place. You can wear your audience out. Spread the participation around. If you have a long presentation, you don't want to see any large gaps where people are sitting and not participating. Also keep in mind that your audience might not be ready to participate immediately, especially if you are presenting at the end of a day when they are tired. Read your audience. Some participation might better be delayed or omitted if your audience does not seem receptive.

And there is nothing in the rulebook that says you need more than one Participation Point. This is not about volume. It's about precision. Choose your moment based on your objective. Have a clear reason for wanting your audience involved at that specific time. You have to be comfortable. If you want, start with only one Participation Point and then add more with each presentation, testing them out and fine-tuning them along the way. Even if your presentation is one minute long, you can still get people involved. You'll even look forward to it. Seriously. It's a lot of fun and you will sense the energy in the room increase—and this is energy you can feed off to increase your own.

Sometimes your audience will get involved without even you knowing it. It might be something your audience will do on their own, or something you created on the spot. Either way, leverage it. Just stay tuned to audience participation and reap the rewards.

Questions/Actions   Positioning

. . . .

. . . .

. . . .

. . . .

. . . .

. . . .

. . . .

. . . .

. . . .

. . . .

Magic Moment

Have you ever been in an audience where all of a sudden everyone look to each other and the energy in the room suddenly explodes? That could very well have been a Magic Moment. You can't miss it. It's like taking a booster cable and jump-staring the enthusiasm in the audience.

This impact can be deliberately created using any number of theatrical devices: the introduction of an unexpected or stunning visual element, the sudden use of music, something incredibly funny causing everyone to laugh, an unusual prop that gets everyone talking. It could also come from audience participation of some kind, such as a demonstration, where everyone in the room is interacting with each other. You can also get a sudden boost of energy by having people stand up to do something.

There is usually just one Magic Moment in a presentation, and it has the beneficial effect of extending your audience's attention span. There is a direct relationship between energy and attention span. If people are tired they take in less information. If they are energized or in this case re-energized, then they can absorb more information. The flip side is that when your information or your delivery of that information is uninspiring, your audience's energy and accompanying attention span will dwindle.

If I may, allow me to share the Magic Moment I created for my *How To Make Hot Cold Calls* seminars. About twenty minutes into my presentation I come to the point where I want to talk about scripting, or what I refer to as the power of words. I want to make the point that my audience's success in booking appointments comes down to just thirty words. This statement alone delivers a lot of impact. When planning my presentation I decided that rather than talk about the point I wanted to make, I wanted my audience to experience it first-hand, and there was no better way for them to do that than by a demonstration of some kind. (Can you sense the participation coming on?) Even though there was another demonstration before this point, and other moments of audience participation, I knew that after this particular point in the presentation there would be a lot of pent-up energy in the room that was just waiting to come out. And I was going to release it. So here's an excerpt from the Magic Moment I created:

"Before we talk about the power of words I'd rather you experience it first. So let's try this simple little demonstration. Look to your left or your right and team up with someone. If anyone doesn't have a partner raise your hands. (A few seconds later after everyone has found a partner I proceed.) I want one of you to play the role of a consultant and the other plays the prospect. When I say 'Go,' and only when I say 'Go,' I want the prospect to ask the consultant this one question: 'You have 30 seconds to tell me why I should do business with you.' Now, I'm going to time you and when thirty seconds is over I'm going to call 'switch!' and then the other person gets to ask you, 'You have 30 seconds to tell me why I should do business with you.' You'll get as good as you gave. Ready? Go!"

I time the audience. At precisely thirty seconds, I continue.

"Switch!"

I time the audience again. After thirty seconds, I continue.

"Stop! Freeze! Time out!" I wait for the audience to be quiet. "Now, hands up, how many people would actually do business with the people next to them based on what they just said?"

"For those of you who put your hands up, there must have been something said that really caught your attention. When you think about it, by the time you open your mouth and introduce yourself to the time you ask for the appointment, you use less than thirty words. That's all. Less then thirty words between you and every opportunity in the world. So what are the thirty words?

Well, they have to be words that hit what I call the

'Greed Glands.' Doctors don't know about it. It's right here on the back of your neck and it makes people say, 'Keep talking, keep talking.' And what activates Greed Glands? It's when you say the very words the person you are talking to wants to hear."

When the audience begins talking in this sudden demonstration the noise level instantly soars (the larger the audience, the louder it gets. You not only hear the energy in the room explode (it's instantaneous), but you can sense a sudden change in body language as people become excited and animated. The room is filled with talk, laughter and emotion. This Magic Moment is a dramatic turning point in the presentation, and a memorable one at that. It's a moment where the audience is completely connected and one hundred per cent involved. Adding to this is a group dynamic where many people are talking to other participants who only moments before were total strangers: they not only made a connection with me; they connected with each other.

Such a moment was all planned and tested. It's my own little surprise for the audience because I know it's coming and they don't.

When you plan your Magic Moment, try to look for ways of getting the audience involved with you and with each other. Look to do something unexpected. Perhaps it has the element of humor or perhaps it is a moment where your presentation builds to a natural climax. For example, back on the first Island of Structure I mentioned this salesperson who impressed me with his product knowledge, espresso machines. In the process of demonstrating some of the machine's features, he actually made a cup of espresso. I can tell you now that the Magic Moment for me came when he handed me the espresso

and told me to enjoy it. This moment was totally unexpected. It was also extremely pleasurable and I must say, very
tasty and refreshing. That Magic Moment summarized his
whole discussion on quality and elevated the experience
because it appealed to my senses of sight, taste, touch and
smell. It then gave us more to talk about, and because I
was very happy, I was all the more willing to listen to anything he had to say.

Some Magic Moments are not planned. They just happen. Sometimes your audience will do something funny in
a demonstration and their anecdotes become the Magic
Moment. While this cannot possibly be anticipated, you
can incorporate the potential for this into your next presentation. Keep your antenna tuned. Don't just watch for
it in your presentation. Look out for Magic Moments in the
presentations of others. When you observe the energy
surge or the focus of others all of a sudden increase, make
a note of how it all happened. Also make a note of where
the Magic Moment occurred and see how timing played a
role. (Would it be any more effective if it came sooner, or
later?) Use and fine-tune what you learn in your own presentation.

Positioning, as you can well imagine, is very important
when designing your Magic Moment. Since the energy
level is going to be significantly elevated, you don't want
to waste it in a part of the presentation where the energy
in the room is already high. Ask yourself what the impact
will be when the energy is piqued at the beginning, middle or end—or anywhere else in between. If you are presenting at the end of a long business day you might need
an energy boost at the very beginning. If your audience is
already a high-energy crowd you might want to hold this
ace close to your chest and play the Magic Moment card
further along in your presentation. Experiment with tim-

ing. Create a Magic Moment in one area of your presentation and then observe the response, and then create another some place else the next time. Once again, self-assess. See where your Magic Moment works best and work it with confidence.

Magic Moment   Positioning

. . . .
. . . .
. . . .
. . . .

Magic Moment   Positioning

. . . .
. . . .
. . . .
. . . .

WOW!

A WOW! is an experience where the audience unexpectedly discovers something interesting, fascinating, or unusual. You can WOW! someone simply by:

- Mentioning a key learning point or insight (sometimes through example), an unusual anecdote, plus facts and figures that people are not expecting.
- Discussing a very compelling unique selling proposition.
- Showing something visually striking.
- Getting the audience participating in a way that is fun and really makes a point come to life.
- Telling a captivating or heart-rending story.
- Offering a new or controversial theory.
- Saying something funny that makes people laugh.

After you deliver a WOW! your audience is thinking, "I didn't know that!" or, "That's really interesting," or "WOW! that looks amazing," or if you get a group reaction one member of the audience might turn to another and say, "Wow! Did you see that?" I'm sure you've had many of those moments when you were a spectator at a good presentation. A WOW! gets people quickly focused and interested in what you are talking about and motivates them to listen further. People seldom forget a WOW! It's what they tend to talk about after a presentation.

A WOW! is something you plan on doing solely to pique people's interest, because when you capture others' interest they get a small boost of energy. Have you ever noticed what happens when you draw with a child using a pencil and then all of a sudden you take out a colored pencil to spice it up? Doesn't the child's attention span suddenly increase when the splash of color is introduced? Isn't the energy level rising?

Here are some interesting differences between a WOW! and a Magic Moment.

Magic Moment:
- Large jolt of energy
- Energy powers audience interest
- Only one Magic Moment in a presentation

WOW!
- Moderate increase in energy
- Interest creates energy
- Lots of opportunities to WOW!

A WOW! is an effective way to regulate both the interest level and the energy level of your audience over the course of your presentation. Say you were reading Little Red Riding Hood to your child. When you get to the part where the wolf cries out, "I'll huff and I'll puff and I'll blowwwwww your house down!" you grab your child and blow on her face and tickle her. Many would consider this a Magic Moment. The only drawback is that you don't know for how long you can keep your audience's attention. But because the impact is huge, dramatic and sudden (not to mention fun), you run the risk of never finishing the story because your child will want you to do it again, and again, and again. Another strategy would be to make a series of interesting comments from time to time as the story unfolds. You might find interesting ways to describe the wolf, you can ask your child what the wolf might be up to next, or just find other ways to get your child involved in the story throughout your reading. You might even have your child read a page or two to aloud. That would be a WOW! strategy because the interest level is maintained consistently with a WOW! around every corner.

The positioning of each WOW! is especially important because you will most likely use several. Since each WOW! piques interest, you have to be very careful not to overwhelm your audience with too many all at once. If you have three unique selling propositions, I'm going to be able to appreciate them more if you tell them to me one at a time with room for my questions and comments in between. If you tell me them all at once, some of them might not register because I might be focused on either the one unique point that caught my attention the most, or the last point you made simply because it was the last and therefore the easiest to remember.

Try to think of a WOW! as a rich chocolate truffle that is meant to be savored. You can easily eat a dozen, but you wouldn't want to do this all at once. It would be a waste. It would be much more enjoyable to savor them one at a time and share the experience with the friend who is serving them. (Friends like that you keep.)

As you serve up each WOW! think about its impact on the audience and decide where it is best positioned. Some WOWs! speak for themselves. Some facts or figures need to accompany the subjects they address. Otherwise simply identify where in your presentation the interest level needs a pick-me-up and then insert your WOW! right there. After your presentation you can always self-assess to see how well it worked. If it worked well, make sure to include it in your next presentation. If it was so-so, then make some enhancement. If it did not deliver the desired effect then scrap it, but before you do, make sure it was the WOW! that was not effective and not its placement. Sometimes the time is all you need to adjust. If you know your audience is full of Type A personalities, then you'll need more WOWs! to keep their attention.

When I speak on *How To Make Hot Cold Calls* I know in advance that when I shatter the sacred cows of telemarketing I always capture my audience's full attention. That's because my theories are controversial. Proven yes, but controversial nonetheless because they are the opposite of what is normally practiced today. Anything controversial gets my audience thinking and asking questions which only helps to generate more interest and energy. Since I can anticipate this rise in energy and interest, I can plan on how to manage it and move it to the point where the audience is hanging on the edge of their chairs waiting for the next sacred cow to be shattered. I'm not offering controversial theories to shock my audience, but rather to enlighten them. When an audience learns something new and profound that will affect their lives or business, you better believe they're going to pay very close attention to your presentation.

So how are you going to WOW! your audience? What are the main points you need to drive home or support? Where do you need people on board? Where does each WOW! belong? After you decide on what and where to WOW! the crowd, write down everything you are saying and doing within five minutes of that point. Do this with every WOW! to make sure it is in the right place and is not going to overwhelm your audience with too much of a good thing. Before we move on, here is one last point: after you create a WOW! make sure that you can explain to yourself exactly what it is about your WOW! that will move your audience. If you can't explain it, it's not going to be effective. When you can identify exactly what will WOW! your audience, look for ways to build on it with things like audience participation or props.

WOW!   Positioning

. . . .

. . . .

. . . .

. . . .

WOW!   Positioning

. . . .

. . . .

. . . .

. . . .

Visual Snapshot

A picture is worth a thousand words, but there is one picture worth ten times as many. It's called your Visual

Snapshot. Here's the difference between visuals (pictures and graphics) and a Visual Snapshot. Ordinary visuals add a level of clarity to any given thought or point. They get the audience thinking, "Oh, I see what you mean." A Visual Snapshot gives clarity to the central theme or point of your discussion and gets the audience thinking, "Oh, I see where we're going with this." This Snapshot is a visual summary of what your presentation is all about.

For this reason, a Visual Snapshot is typically found either at the beginning of a presentation or at the beginning of a section or both. You can have just one main Snapshot summarizing the whole presentation or a series of them summarizing each main section, but even then there is always one predominant visual. The Visual Snapshot acts as a road map for you too because it helps you instantly crystallize your thoughts. That's why it's a good idea to focus on your Snapshots before you present.

A good Visual Snapshot helps people instantly and completely UNDERSTAND and RELATE to the subject you are presenting. The more interesting your Snapshot, the more your audience will WANT TO listen further and give you their undivided attention. It is also cheap insurance to secure the attention of Type A personalities who need to see in the first few seconds exactly where all this is going.

I put a visual road map in the first section of this book, where the fundamentals are listed. Do you recall the Snapshot? It was the ladder with the words "Have To" on the bottom and "Want To" on the top. That Visual Snapshot defines the underlying philosophy of this system, which is that people don't buy from you because they have to, people buy from you because they want to, and it's your job to know how to get them in a WANT TO frame of mind. With this knowledge in mind, I wanted to create a single visual that would sum up my main point. The ladder came to mind because I was asking myself how people climb up the evolutionary ladder from HAVE TO to WANT TO. Without any notes whatsoever I can talk around that visual for hours. It provides clarity and absolute focus to the discussion.

Your Visual Snapshot can be a pure visual without words, or one like my ladder with a few words. It can also contain a heading or slogan with no pictures or graphics whatsoever. It could be as simple as a chart showing the potential impact of your product on your customer's sales. One of my clients wanted to give a presentation about a new service that would eliminate the need for customers to pay penalties on late payments. His Visual Snapshot was very creative. My client scanned a government tax form and superimposed a heading that read: "Taxes are inevitable. Penalties are not." The point was made instantly and graphically.

If you could summarize your entire presentation in a single visual, what would it be? Here are few things to think about to help you get those creative juices flowing:

What is the central theme or main premise of your presentation?

. . . .
. . . .

What does the central theme remind you of?

. . . .
. . . .

What does the central theme look like, sound like, taste like, smell like, feel like?

. . . .
. . . .

What is the underlying philosophy?

. . . .
. . . .

What is your audience's life like without your product—
and what is life like with your product?

. . . .
. . . .

What do you want your presentation to accomplish?

. . . .
. . . .

What is the most memorable part of your presentation?

. . . .
. . . .

What is the most unusual or controversial point you are
making?

. . . .
. . . .

What is the most unique aspect of the subject you are
discussing?

. . . .
. . . .

What do you want your audience to remember more
than anything else?

. . . .
. . . .
. . . .
. . . .
. . . .

What will your audience need to UNDERSTAND in order to take action?

. . . .
. . . .
. . . .
. . . .

Now translate those observations into an interesting Visual Snapshot:

Visuals

Outside your main Visual Snapshot there will be all kinds of visuals you probably want to include in your presentation, whether they are photos of people and places, graphics of every description, or charts and diagrams with facts, figures and estimates and all that good stuff. Visuals are important because they clarify a point and help your audience UNDERSTAND. Some people communicate best when they use visuals to express their thoughts, and others learn best when they are taught with visuals. I myself think visually and then write to the visuals in my mind. People who need visuals to learn rely on them to hold their attention. A good visual makes a point come to life. It helps your audience RELATE to your message. An interesting visual also makes your point and your presentation memorable.

Somewhere in the evolution of presentations people got a little crazy with visuals. For some reason, visuals have become the focus of the presentation rather than a reinforcement. Visuals and graphics are only tools. They are not the whole show. How many times have you sat through a presentation where the presenter spent a fortune on fancy graphics and visuals but you were bored to death because there was no substance in the message, or the presenter had no passion for the delivery? Don't hide behind your visuals. You are the leading actor and your visuals are the supporting cast.

At the end of the day the product is you.

Back in my advertising days one of the first things I learned was that in print advertising the graphics should never overpower the message. The copy carried the substance, and the visuals either made the copy stand out or drew attention to the advertisement.

Each and every visual you use should be chosen for a reason. A very good reason. They should be used to make or clarify a point only when the point is an important or pivotal one. A visual can have a picture or illustration of something, or just a few words. Whichever is the case, make it interesting and make sure you can talk at length about the subject matter of your visual. An effective visual opens the mind to other thoughts and questions. It encourages dialogue.

If you have a slide with a lot of text or details, try to keep it to no more than six bullets of copy with each bullet containing approximately six to eight words. Short and sweet is the rule. How many times have you seen slides where you have to sit there and read them for a few minutes each, or worse, sit there while the presenter reads them for you word for word? Who needs the presenter in that case? When you have a lot of information to go over, cover the highlights on your visuals and then talk about them in greater detail. If required, leave your audience with a handout covering the other details.

Try to be creative with your visuals. The most interesting visuals are the ones you least expect to see. If you were a roofer you could show a picture of the homes you have worked on and talk about the variety of structures you have experience working with. You can make it even more interesting by showing a picture of the Navajo Desert. Nobody is expecting that one. All you have to do is say to your audience, "The Navajo Desert is one of the driest places under the sun. The other ones are under my roofs." They will never forget the visual, and with it the knowledge that hiring your services means leak-free roofs. In this example, you noticed that the visual was not the product but the effect of the product. The main benefit, if you will.

By the way, don't forget that you can elevate the power of your visuals with a dose of audience participation. You can have someone else show the visuals, or you can ask questions about the visuals to get your audience not only involved, but also thinking about the points you are bringing to life.

To help you decide what visuals will impress your audience, here's a few questions to answer:

What are the main points of discussion?

. . . .
. . . .

What points of discussion need to be simplified?

. . . .
. . . .

What is the main impression you want to make on the audience?

. . . .
. . . .

What is the single most important thought you want your audience to remember?

. . . .
. . . .

What is the main benefit of your products/services?

. . . .
. . . .

When you are ready to create a list of visuals, make note of where you want them placed. If you plan on using one to support a point, you can use that visual either before, during or after you make your point: if you showed your visual first it could act as a teaser to get your audience thinking about the point you are about to make; when you introduce your visual during a point you are making, it simply adds instant clarity; should you use the visual after a point, it might be by way of an example of some kind. I would like you to also consider how each of your visuals relates to the other Spices you so diligently created. For example, a visual can be part of a WOW! or a demonstration. If you want to use a visual to follow a WOW!, make sure that it builds on the moment rather than distracting from the energy and excitement the WOW! just created.

Visual   Positioning

. . . .
. . . .
. . . .
. . . .

Visual   Positioning

. . . .
. . . .
. . . .
. . . .

Props

Remember the example of the roofer with the Navajo Desert picture? If the roofer wanted to make his presentation even more memorable, all he would have to do is hand his audience actual samples of his shingles. People would be more involved and connected because they would be using more of their senses. Instead of just seeing a picture they could feel the weight and texture of each type of shingle. The shingle would become a prop.

It seems that the minute I talk about props some people get a gut reaction that tells them "I can't use props. I'm not a circus act." People seem to have a natural hesitation to using props, and that's a shame because any performer can tell you that props can really make a performance shine.

A prop is nothing more than an object, which is used to illustrate a point. Think of a prop as a 3-D visual that you can hold in your hand. People can see props, touch them, feel them, smell them, taste them and hear them. The prop creates an experience, which makes your presentation more memorable. They enable people to quickly RELATE to your points. A great prop should also elevate audience participation. No wonder props are terrific enhancements to any demonstration or example you provide.

You probably won't use more than one or two props in any given presentation. Since props are dramatic by their very presence, use them sparingly and carefully just like you would with any other visual. Props do not need to be big or complicated. They can be as simple as a paper clip or a pen. More important than the prop itself is how you use it.

I told you a while back about my business card that looks and feels like a playing card (the ace of spades). It makes a good first impression because it demonstrates my creativity. But more important than that is how I use the card as a prop. When someone asks for my card I reach into my breast pocket and pull out a regular deck of cards. All the while I say nothing and just look the person in the eye with a smile. I can see the surprised look on the person's face. I open the deck, fan the cards and then cut the deck in one hand, at which point my business card appears on top. (I had prepared the deck beforehand by placing my business card in the middle of the other regular cards.) At that point I take the card with my other hand and as I present it to my audience, I simply say, "My card." Presentation is everything.

Since a prop is visual, you will have to give a fair bit of thought as to how you are going to present it. You need to set up the prop with the right lead-in line and then follow it with a punch line if appropriate. For the sake of a simple example, suppose you are a sales manager addressing your sales team. Your talk is on how you will help your salespeople reach their targets so they can make their bonus this quarter. You can make your point come alive with a good prop, but the question is, which prop? How do you figure out which one to use? Start by looking at your objective or the main theme of your discussion. In this example it would be their targets, so what comes to mind when you think of targets?

> A target is something you aim at…
> …it's round with lots of circles…
> …what is the most famous target of all?…
> …William Tell, hmmmmmm…
> …he used to aim at apples…
> …apples!

With props in hand you call a meeting of your staff in the boardroom. When they enter they see a shiny red apple in front of each seat. The visual impact is fairly obvious and immediate. Nice icebreaker. You then begin the meeting by saying, "William Tell never missed a target and I want to help you reach yours."

What if you were a plumbing supply distributor and you wanted to let your prospective customers know that you distribute all across the continent. A prop in this example can be as simple as a map of North America, but if you want to be a little different, create a map without any borders. That visual will open up a conversation about a seamless network of distributors.

What if you were in the insurance business and the opportunity you were sharing was the ability to protect your clients from lost income when they are ill. A watch could be a terrific prop. It's certainly on hand at a moment's notice. Here's how you could set it up:

> You look at your watch and then take it off to show your client. "I've had this watch for most of my life." (Pause for a moment as you place the watch in your customer's hand.) "It can always tell me what time it is but it can't tell me what's going to happen in the next minute. That's why I feel strongly that being prepared for any uncertainties is always in your best interest."

As you can see by these basic examples, a prop can be a simple, everyday item. It's all in how you present it. I strongly urge you to use a prop in your next presentation. Start with something simple but set it up right and have a good punch line to tie it to your message. The more your audience interacts with the prop, the more memorable the experience. Even simply holding the prop in their hands will give them a stronger connection with your message. Whatever you do, don't make a big deal of the props when you use them. Your delivery should be very casual and nonchalant. You have to be sincere—the point you want to make must get the respect it deserves. The very presence of a prop is strong enough that it never needs to be overplayed. It is not there for entertainment.

Your prop is there to make an important point. When presenting a prop, always take your dear sweet time. Like presenting a fine wine, the experience should never be rushed.

Take a moment and complete the following exercise that will help you create and present your next prop.

What is the point you need to make with the prop? What do you want it to achieve?

. . . .
. . . .

Look at your answer above and write down what it reminds you of.

. . . .
. . . .

Take whatever it reminds you of and think of any visual associations.

. . . .
. . . .

What props can be used to demonstrate those visuals?

. . . .
. . . .

What is the patter that will accompany it?
How you set up the scenario:

. . . .
. . . .
. . . .
. . . .
. . . .
. . . .

What you say as you show and use the prop:

. . . .
. . . .
. . . .
. . . .
. . . .
. . . .

Your punch line:

. . . .
. . . .
. . . .
. . . .

How do you and your audience interact with the prop?

. . . .
. . . .
. . . .
. . . .
. . . .

Start with one simple prop and then add more as your experience grows. You will know when your prop has had the desired effect because you will see the expression on the faces of your audience. You are still reading your audience, aren't you? Self-assess after your presentation. Incorporate the elements that went well, including any good adlibs that your audience comes up with. If something needs adjusting, it might be the prop, the way it was handled, your segue into the prop or your punch line. Make the adjustment and then retest. When you end up with a polished presentation of a prop, it will always be one of the highlights of your presentation, for you and your audience.

Prop	Positioning
. . . .	
. . . .	
. . . .	

Prop	Positioning
. . . .	
. . . .	
. . . .	

As we come to the end of the Spice section, there is one last finishing touch you need to add. After you have filled the spice rack with all the assorted Spices, incorporate them into the main body of your presentation, which you last adjusted when you mixed in your bridges. You will know which Spices go where because you have already earmarked their positioning. The main body of your presentation will now be in its final form.

Delivery

Once the final structure of your presentation is in place, how are you going to stand before your audience and deliver it? Up to this point we have concentrated on the content because even a great delivery can't make up for a loss of substance. After all, people are going to buy from you because of the strength and merits of your proposition. Besides, if your audience does not UNDERSTAND or RELATE to your message, your delivery will fall on deaf ears. You can go to the theater and watch a well-written play, but if the performance is not good, the words never come to life. You have the power to captivate your audience by the way you present.

A presentation by its very nature is a performance. You have an audience, remember? That makes you a performer and every performer worth his or her salt pays a great deal of attention to lines they deliver. Now I better stop here for a second just in case you have some apprehension about performing. This is not as formal as it sounds.

Performing simply means that you are going to prepare and rehearse the way you deliver your content, and then speak with passion, conviction and enthusiasm. Just as you have a formal structure to your presentation content, there is a process for ensuring that your words and your meaning are well received. You don't have to be a gifted performer or have tons of charisma to enthrall an audience. So kick up your feet and follow me along on this one.

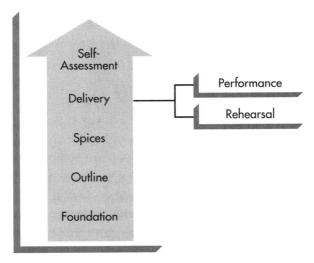

To set the stage for our discussion, I need to point out that the art of delivering a compelling presentation is an art unto itself, and there are many excellent books on this subject. I don't feel I can add anything to the work that is already out there, with the exception of helping you execute effectively some of the fundamentals of presentation delivery. In particular, I will focus on helping you better UNDERSTAND the main drivers behind a compelling delivery, especially the discipline of rehearsing. I also want to talk about how to overcome any fear, apprehension or nervousness you might have when presenting in front of an audience.

A case for content

My years of experience have taught me that the foundation of any great delivery remains the content. If your content is not interesting, why on earth would you want to deliver it? On the other hand, content that inspires you also inspires your audience. I've said before that the words you speak paint images in people's minds, and people move in the images you create. But you also move in the images you create. So before you present, take the time to reflect back on your storyline. A good story is always worth telling.

The role of product knowledge

People will only have confidence in you if you know what you are talking about. The basis of knowing what you are talking about is knowing what you are selling. I know we talked about product knowledge earlier when we had a discussion about first impressions, but it bears some repeating here. If you don't know everything about your products and services, then you can't effectively answer questions and there goes that trust right out the window. When you know your product, you can answer questions effectively and stay in control. Product knowledge gives you confidence because you know you will be able to talk intelligently about your offerings. Product knowledge also enables you to more thoroughly plan your demonstrations and examples because you will know exactly what needs demonstrating and the kinds of examples that your audience needs.

What's behind the passion

Your appreciation of the value you bring to the table will enable you to believe in the opportunity you present. This belief not only builds confidence, it is also the engine behind the passion with which you speak. Passion also comes from enjoying your own presentation either because it's interesting or just plain fun. When you look forward to the presentation, your enthusiasm will come out naturally, it will spill over your audience. Let's warm up that passion a little.

What is it about the opportunity you are sharing that excites you?

. . . .
. . . .
. . . .

What is it about this opportunity that excites your customers?

. . . .
. . . .

What is the biggest value customer's will receive?

. . . .
. . . .
. . . .

What part of your presentation are you really looking forward to?

. . . .
. . . .

If for any reason you cannot answer these questions just yet, you are not ready to present. There has to be value. Otherwise, why would someone buy it? You need to identify the value and be able to articulate it. If you can't find anything exciting about your presentation, you need to add some Spices.

By the way, just because you speak passionately does not mean that you have to speak in a hurry. Your presentations should never, ever sound rushed. Take your time. If you only have a short period of time, then create a presentation that you can deliver without rushing. (Work within the time parameters you identified in your presentation objectives.) When you rush you give the impression that you are not prepared or confident. You don't sound as though what you have to say is important. Have you ever heard royalty rush their words? There are times when you will deliberately want to speak more quickly, but overall, make sure people have time to absorb the meaning of your words and the images these words create. When you are practicing your presentation, pay close attention to your overall pacing and tone. You should sound passionate, confident in your subject matter, approachable (so that people will feel comfortable asking you questions), energetic and above all, natural. Be yourself. Imagine the person you are presenting to is a friend, and you are excited about sharing a really wonderful opportunity with that friend. Your tone should be no different than as if this really was the case.

Rehearsing

Rehearsing is essential to a flawless delivery. There is no way you can wing it and be perfect unless you are either lucky or a naturally gifted performer, but even seasoned professionals rehearse and rehearse and rehearse. Can you imagine showing up at the theater one evening when the performers didn't have time to rehearse? Not only would the show be a dud, you would feel cheated of the time and money you invested. When you are giving a presentation, your audience deserves the best. Period.

When you are prepared and polished, you are effective.

Just as important, you are showing respect: respect for your audience, respect for the opportunity you are presenting and respect for yourself.

Rehearsing is a confidence booster because nothing is left to chance. It's one thing to feel good about your content and your delivery; it's another to feel completely confident in your ability to be effective with each and every presentation. Rehearsing is a true prerequisite for success. I've never heard of anyone not having a great presentation or sales call because that person was too prepared. Rehearsing reminds me of the best lesson I was taught in life. It came from the Boy Scouts and their famous motto: "Be prepared!" I can promise you from experience, preparation always comes through for you.

Rehearsing has another interesting side effect: it enables you to deliver a flawless performance at a moment's notice. This is particularly handy when you are networking or when a customer drops by without an appointment and you find yourself having to give a quick presentation. It is also the best insurance for those times when you are not feeling well. There have been numerous occasions when I was coming down with something but could not cancel a seminar that hundreds of people were going out of their way to attend. When your body aches and your mind is cloudy, the ability to have your thoughts go on autopilot is a blessing. The countless rehearsals I did enabled my mouth to deliver all my thoughts even though my mind had long gone home to bed with a hot tea and lemon.

I remember giving a one-hour speech a few years back in front of 120 executives at the Association for Corporate Growth. That particular evening I was coming down with some kind of flu. All I knew was that I felt like a two-volt battery and even that bit of energy was leaving me fast. Before the speech I focused on how my material was going to be a big help to my audience; that gave me a shot of adrenaline so my energy crisis would not be an issue. About halfway into my presentation my mind went blank because of the condition I was in. (Mayday! Mayday!) I wasn't worried because I knew that since I had rehearsed this presentation a million times (that is four rehearsals short of an exaggeration) I could get back on track immediately once I knew where I left off. So rather than get frustrated and risk losing my audience by going off on a tangent, I stopped and simply asked the following:

> "Do you ever get one of those moments when your mind goes blank because your thoughts were five minutes ahead of what you are talking about?"
> Everyone nodded in agreement.
> "Well I'm having one of those moments right now. Where was I?"
> Everyone smiled, along with a few chuckles, and well over twenty people hollered where I had left off. I was then able to continue, knowing that my audience was very much connected with me.

Now here's the funny part. After the speech a number of the presidents in the audience came up to me and said that they thought it was really clever how I tested them to see if they were listening. I didn't have the heart to spoil their fun by telling them that I really did lose my train of thought. On occasion I now stop in a meeting, pretend my mind goes blank and ask what my last thought was. It always tells me how much of what I'm saying is really soaking in.

How To Rehearse

Rehearsing requires that you practice your presentation on your own or with a colleague or a friend, but not in front of a prospect or a real customer.

Rehearsing is habit-forming and requires discipline. I remember giving a one-hour seminar for the International Customer Service Association, and a person who identified herself as a professional speaker came up to me afterward to tell me how much she enjoyed it. Commenting on the fact that I did not read from notes, she said, "Tell me you've done this a thousand times before." "I haven't," I answered. "It's called rehearsing." I once told someone that the sign of a true champion is someone who rehearses even when that person doesn't feel like rehearsing. This holds true with most athletes.

A rehearsal is not one activity, but rather a series of things you do within a period of time. The activities are designed to get you to the point where you are completely comfortable with your material, and you can talk about it conversationally and passionately. It's much like going to the gym to work out. You don't do everything all at once, and you don't lift all the heaviest weights first. You warm up your muscles first and then follow a routine that slowly builds to the point where you have completed all your exercises with the maximum results.

The first thing to do is pick a location where you can rehearse without distractions. It doesn't matter if it's in your home, office or outside. I myself prefer to go for long walks down a country road near Lake Wilcox to rehearse my seminars. The road takes about one hour to complete on a return trip which gives me just enough time to talk through one seminar. There is a horse at the end of the road that I love to visit, but if I get talking about horses we'll never finish our discussion. The first point I want to make is to rehearse not just where it's comfortable, but where it's inspiring. If the weather is nice take your computer out on your deck and rehearse. An inspiring background will give you energy and generate great results.

Once you choose your location, don't jump into your presentation right away. You have to warm up to it, just like you do at the gym. First clear your mind of all the other stuff that's clogging your thoughts. For the first five minutes just enjoy the scenery. If you are indoors, think about some of the fun parts of the presentation that you are looking forward to. After you have warmed up, give your mind a rehearsal road map by visualizing the storyline. This will give you the big picture. It will tell you where your rehearsal will be going. Then proceed to verbalize the opening minute. Don't perfect your opening minute just yet. Just verbalize it for now so you get familiar with it. Speaking out loud is an integral part of rehearsing. When you hear your own words repeatedly spoken, they tend to better stick in your memory. By hearing your delivery you can also pay attention to things like pacing, emphasis and energy. It also enables you to use your body language in real time as you go through the motions of a real presentation.

A simple way to quickly learn your opening minute is to rehearse it in bite-size pieces, beginning with your opening line. For example, suppose that the line below was your opening line:

Every second of every day you can witness with your own eyes the movement of goods and people across this vast continent.

Just below I have chopped it up into pieces that are easier to remember. Say the first line until you can deliver it without reading it, and then proceed to the next in the same fashion. As you do this, place emphasis on the words in italics.

> Every second of every day.
> Every second of every day *you can witness.*
> Every second of every day you can witness *with your own eyes.*
> Every second of every day you can witness with your own eyes *the movement of goods and people.*
> Every second of every day you can witness with your own eyes the movement of goods and people *across this vast continent.*
> Every second of every day you can witness with your own eyes the movement of goods and people across this vast continent.

Continue this exercise with the rest of your opening minute.

Next, very quickly verbalize each of your bridges. You recall we spoke about bridges in the Spices section; they're the crucial segues that connect one section of your presentation to another. Bridges are like the frame of a house; they define the rooms and form the structure on which you build. The rooms here would be the various sections of your presentation. It's important to thoroughly rehearse your bridges so that your mind can fill each room with content. By practicing these connecting thoughts you get a quick feel for the natural sequence of events in your presentation. It's like getting familiar with the rhythm of a song; you might not know all the words but you can tap your feet to the beat. By repeating your bridges in quick succession you are turning them into a reflex, which your mind can respond to without even thinking about it.

There is a sequence to rehearsing your bridges. Begin by verbalizing your first bridge. Then repeat it and continue to your second bridge. Next, start again with your first bridge, followed by your second bridge and then add your third. Next time build on this same sequence. First bridge, second bridge, third bridge, fourth bridge etc.

Bridge 1.
Bridge 1 and 2.
Bridge 1 and 2 and 3.
Bridge 1 and 2 and 3 and 4.

Continue this process until all your bridges have been verbalized. This process constantly reinforces the relationship between the bridges, and in doing so engraves the natural sequence of your presentation in your mind. After rehearsing your bridges, verbalize your ending (closing thoughts and closing line). Then repeat this process from opening minute to bridges to the ending a few times until it seems effortless.

Opening minute.
Bridge 1.
Bridge 1 and 2.
Bridge 1 and 2 and 3.
Bridge 1 and 2 and 3 and 4, etc.
Ending.

That was your warm-up.

Now that you are comfortable with the rhythm of your presentation, take a look at the main body and rehearse each section one at a time. If you don't have distinct sections, then artificially divide your main thoughts into sections based on time. For example, if your presentation is only ten minutes long, divide it into five sections of two minutes each or two sections of five minutes each. The idea is to rehearse in small pieces so you can concentrate on one area at a time, proceeding to the next area only when you feel confident. Imagine a selection of delicious hors d'oeuvres laid out on a table. Instead of piling them on your plate and then eating them all at once, take one and savor it all alone, enjoying its texture, design and taste. Then do the same for each hors d'oeuvre. You should do this when you rehearse each section. Don't rush through them without thinking about what you are saying. Take the time to think about the message you are delivering and the meaning of the words you speak.

Before you rehearse a section, ask yourself the following questions:

What is the main thought I want to get across in this section?

. . . .
. . . .

What kind of Spices am I using to reinforce my ideas?

. . . .
. . . .

What is the most powerful metaphor in this section?

. . . .
. . . .

What is the most memorable part of this section?

. . . .
. . . .
. . . .
. . . .

What is my favorite part in this section?

. . . .

. . . .

Focusing on the answers to these questions moves you from a point of just memorizing your thoughts (where you don't necessarily think about what you are saying), to a deeper state of internalizing the true message you want to convey. Proceed to answer these questions for each section you review.

Section 1.
Section 2.
Section 3.
Section 4.
Section 5.

Once you have completed all your sections separately, go back and rehearse them together as one cohesive presentation with the opening minute, all the bridges and the ending.

Opening minute.
Section 1.
Bridge.
Section 2.
Bridge.
Section 3.
Bridge.
Section 4.
Bridge.
Section 5.
Ending.

After you have successfully rehearsed the entire main body of your presentation, go back and rehearse this section's *out of sequence*. For example, start with Section 1, then skip to Section 5, then go back to section 3, then 2, then 4 etc. This is a separate exercise designed to make sure that you have mastered your material. If you don't know any part of your presentation you will get all mixed up during the jumping back and forth. If you know your stuff, you will rehearse each section without missing anything. Leave out the bridges for now because it will require all your focus just to concentrate on all the disjointed sections.

Section 1.
Section 5.
Section 3.
Section 2.
Section 4.

Once you have successfully completed this exercise a few times, try it with the bridges, only instead of using the bridge that comes at the end of a Section, use the bridge that precedes a section because your next section will now be out of sequence.

Section 1.
Bridge to #5.
Section 5.
Bridge to #3.
Section 3.
Bridge to #2.
Section 2.
Bridge to #4.
Section 4.

This exercise sharpens your focus because it forces you to think very hard and very quickly about your material. You will find that your earlier rehearsal on bridges will pay off here because it will be the bridges that make it easier for you to jump quickly from one section to another.

When you have done this last exercise to your satisfaction, go back and rehearse the entire presentation from start to finish *in sequence*; you should now notice that you breezed through the material much easier this time around.

Opening minute.
Section 1.
Bridge.
Section 2.
Bridge.
Section 3.
Bridge.
Section 4.
Bridge.
Section 5.
Ending.

At this point feel free to take a break. This is not a marathon. Besides, I want you to enjoy it. The next part of rehearsing is actually a lot of fun. Up until this point the purpose of your rehearsal has been to make sure that you know your material forward and backward, right side in and inside out. Your confidence is building nicely. Now you are ready to work on the actual delivery of the material.

Let's get your energy up. Think about your favorite part of the presentation. It might be a story, example, demonstration, perhaps a Magic Moment or WOW! You might have several parts you are excited about. Whatever they are, rehearse them for a minute, just for the fun of it.

Next, rehearse your use of props. Other than being fun (which they are), props need separate attention because your patter must be smooth and your handling of a prop has to be flawless. You have to be comfortable using props and you have to look comfortable using them. The more familiar you become with props, the more casual you will look in presenting them. Make sure to practice the ways you will handle the props. Practice also the ways your audience will handle them. If possible, practice in front of a mirror. This gives you an instant audience to practice in front of (with a familiar face no less), and also enables you to see how you look from your audience's vantage point.

Proceed to rehearse your demonstrations if applicable. Here too your patter is as essential as the handling of any props or the use of audience participation. Be sure to rehearse everything you want people to see, do, touch and experience. This is the time to practice using all your audiovisual aids as well. If you are using slides, rehearse the timing of your patter with the timing of the visuals so you are not interrupting your presentation looking for the next visual.

At this point you are ready to look at the quality of your delivery. This time rehearse your pacing and enunciation. Make sure every word is clearly spoken and unhurried. Pay particular attention to your opening minute and your closing minute. If you are addressing a Type A personality or you naturally speak quickly, you can pick up the pace any time as soon as your opening minute has passed. But under no circumstances should your opening line be hurried. It must always be slow and deliberate because that first minute sets the direction and tone of the presentation. It is a focus point for both you and your audience, and if you go too fast the focus becomes blurred and you disconnect from the audience. Your closing minute needs to be nice and slow because, here too, you need your audience to pay attention to every word. It's your ending that brings the presentation full circle and ultimately moves your audience to take action.

Practice your pacing first with the opening and closing minutes before proceeding to the main body. Try recording your opening and closing, either with a tape recorder or through your voice mail. When you play it back, it should sound like a presentation from someone who is confident. If you sound hurried in any way go back and do it again until all your words are said deliberately and unhurriedly. While you are recording, also listen very carefully to make sure that you sound completely conversational. If you want to put down your main body verbatim, first write it conversationally and then deliver it in the same manner. Always remember that a presentation is simply a conversation about a specific topic of interest. Talk to your audience as though you are talking to people over lunch, rather than in an office or from behind a podium.

It's also a good idea to clock your presentation so you know you can finish in time. I strongly recommend that you time each individual section so when you are actually presenting, you can tell how much time you have left without having to look at your watch.

You are now ready for the ultimate in fine-tuning. I'm assuming that you don't plan on speaking in monotone. Your voice will have natural inflections. But certain thoughts will warrant special attention. Identify key phrases and words you need to emphasize. This is a strategic decision. Look for thoughts that are pivotal to the understanding of your topic, or areas where people need to really concentrate. When you write your presentation out,

either word for word, or in point form, underline or bold-
face the words you want to emphasize. In *How To Make
Hot Cold Calls* I refer to this as script encoding. Take a
word you want to draw attention to and practice raising
your pitch, raising the volume, lowering the volume,
stretching the word out (i.e. more becomes morrrrrre) or
pausing for a half second. Pausing is extremely powerful
and should only be used on a selective basis. When you
pause at the right moment you command your audience's
undivided attention. You will control the moment.

I'm not sure if you are more comfortable reading from
notes, but as a rule I don't use them. The flow is more natural. The rapport with the audience is always better when
you connect with people through direct eye contact.

Instead of reading notes, read your audience.

Talking directly to your audience sends a message that you
know your material inside out. Having said all this, if you
still feel that you need notes, practice reading from them
so you don't lose your place while giving a demonstration
or using a prop. If possible, keep your notes to a minimum
by just referring to your bridges, some key points or essential facts and figures.

By the time you complete the rehearsal process you
just learned, you will be more than ready for your dress
rehearsal. What? No one told you about that? Well go on,
get dressed. Yeah, I know you're dressed, but I want you in
the exact clothes you will be wearing for your presentation. If you are going to speak the part you have to look
the part. While you are at it, gather up all the equipment
you'll be using. A dress rehearsal means a complete run-
through of the entire presentation with visuals, props,
computers—everything. Time your dress rehearsal and

compare it with the time you kept in your last rehearsal. You need to finish exactly on time. Not a minute past. When people are expecting a five-minute presentation, they tend to get annoyed if you talk past the allotted time. Once you set an expectation, you have to deliver. If for some reason in your final rehearsal your timing is off (too short or too long), then make adjustments, beginning with those elements which are easier to lengthen or shorten, such as demonstrations or audience participation.

Rehearsing is a routine once you get used to it. You will feel a lot more confident going into any presentation having invested the time to get it right. The results will speak for themselves. I hope you enjoy rehearsing because here's something you're really going to love: no sooner do you finish rehearsing and give your presentation then it's time to rehearse all over again. That's right. Every presentation has to be rehearsed—even the ones you have already given. If you are giving a presentation for the first time, practice will make perfect. If you are giving the same presentation for the second, third or hundredth time, rehearsal is just as essential to your success as if it were the very first time. If there is a significant length of time between your presentations you might get rusty and forget key elements of your delivery, and if you make changes to your presentation they will need to be rehearsed too.

Your hundredth presentation has to be as fresh and dynamic as your first. It might be *your* tenth time but it's the first time for your audience. They deserve the best performance.

Obviously if it's the first time you are giving a particular presentation, you will need more rehearsals, and longer ones at that, to get it perfect. For those presentations you give often you will need less practice because there is less time to practice. When I first started rehearsing my professional seminars, I would practice several hours a day for a month. After that my rehearsal time was reduced to a few hours a week and eventually down to a few hours per month. If I have a speaking engagement in the meantime, I still practice several times before that particular performance. The consistency of practicing keeps me fresh, and enables me to reduce the practice time required before a show.

All the practice in the world won't pay off if you don't take the time before your presentation to focus on what you are presenting, to whom and why. Focus enables you to think clearly and speak passionately. Focus gives you control, and control, as you know by now, means confidence.

Before I give any speech or seminar I do a technique very similar to the Pot of Gold technique I teach in *How To Make Hot Cold Calls*. I take a few minutes to focus on the value I'm bringing to the table and how people will be better off for this experience. I then picture myself in front of my audience and visualize the presentation unfolding. I see my audience asking questions and me responding. This way, when they do ask questions, my mind can go on autopilot and answer them without hesitation. I picture my Magic Moment, which gets me all excited because I really look forward to it. I proceed to envision myself delivering my closing line nice and slow with impact and the audience applauding. If it's a presentation for a sales call, I will also visualize someone raising an objection and how my well-prepared response turns the person around. I then picture my prospect going for the Final Close by asking me "Steven, where do we go from here?" Whether I'm giving a speech or a sales presentation, I will then picture myself as a member of the audience looking *at me* presenting to the group. This enables me to feel what the audience feels, and see what the audience sees. By placing myself in the role of a participant, I connect with my audience instantly because in my mind, for that brief moment, I am one of them. You may recall that this is much the same reason why I make sure to shake hands with my audience before each presentation.

I do all this visualization before I leave my office. When I'm giving a seminar or speech I will deliberately go off to another room to close my eyes and run through what I just described. The image I put in my mind at that moment will set my mind on the right course. In other words, the picture I see is the performance I will deliver.

The Butterflies

Your ability to focus before a presentation will also help you overcome any fear, apprehension or nervousness. Have you ever had butterflies in your stomach before you go on? That's a perfectly natural response even if you love presenting. It's healthy because it is pent-up excitement and anticipation. This is not to be confused with stage fright. There is a difference between feeling butterflies or looking for the exit sign. I would like to share with you my seven-step remedy for overcoming fear, apprehension and the butterflies. If you only have butterflies, skip the first step.

1. Begin by taking ownership of your fear or apprehension. Right now you probably have a negative image in your mind that is leaving your subconscious with no other option. So take a moment and draw what comes to mind when you see yourself presenting.

Describe how you feel when you present:

. . . .
. . . .
. . . .
. . . .
. . . .

If you were not afraid or apprehensive about making presentations, how would you feel? What would be different?

. . . .
. . . .
. . . .
. . . .
. . . .

Now, if your audience was to describe the best presenter they ever saw, what would they say?

. . . .
. . . .
. . . .
. . . .
. . . .

If you were the best presenter your audience ever saw, draw what you would look like.

Now you have a positive image to focus on, and one your mind will move toward.

2. The less confident you are about your presentation, the greater your angst. When you are prepared and well

rehearsed, you have nothing to worry about. You will go on autopilot the moment your audience begins because you have practiced and practiced and practiced and practiced. (Hey, you can't practice enough.) If you have time before you head off to your presentation, take a short rehearsal of just the highlights.

3. Before the presentation, think very carefully about the value you are bringing to the table and the impact your presentation will have on your audience. Articulate your value proposition. By saying the words out loud you create images that will inspire you and get your passion flowing.

4. Then walk yourself through your opening minute. Don't just verbalize it. Picture yourself presenting it in front of your audience. This constructive focus on the opening line blocks out other distractions, which only serve to increase anxiety by cluttering your mind. All you should be thinking about seconds before your presentation is your opening line. Once you deliver it you will have warmed up, read your audience and started rolling along just like you rehearsed.

5. Just before you go on, take a few deep, slow breaths from your diaphragm. This is incredibly effective at relaxing your body and clearing your mind. It helps you focus and gives you one more layer of control.

6. If you are presenting to a large audience, before you begin your presentation look directly at a few people so you see individuals instead of a faceless crowd. This will help personalize your approach; you instantly sound more conversational and strike an immediate rapport with your

audience because you will sound like you are talking directly to each person. As your presentation unfolds, make sure you make direct eye contact with everyone. Even when I am presenting in front of a thousand people, I make sure to address individuals in the front, back, middle and everywhere in between.

When you connect with everyone, everyone connects with you.

7. The moment you see the audience smile, laugh, acknowledge that they are listening, or participate in any way, you will feel a connection with them, and that acceptance should make any remaining butterflies migrate south.

Self-Assessment

Your delivery will become more effective over time not only because of all the rehearsing you do, but also from applying what you learn after each presentation. As simple as it sounds, what I'm referring to is an important behavioral change that requires practice. It's called self-assessment. This is the ability to identify where a mistake was made and the problems it caused in order to prevent it from ever happening again. In my book of life, it's fine to make mistakes; that's how we learn. It's not OK to make the same mistake twice.

If your presentation is not successful, you have the responsibility to find out what needs fixing and make the necessary changes before you deliver it again. The presentation process you have just learned will give you the ability to identify areas for improvement and enables you to make necessary changes in the minimum amount of time. You might have come across a new question or objection for which you either did not have an answer or a good answer. You might need to move some information to an earlier slot because people were asking questions about material that you planned to discuss later in your presentation. If you experienced a disconnect from your audience you will need to make sure that whatever you were discussing at that moment will be clearer the next time. There might have been a new buying signal you overlooked.

When your presentation is successful, self-assess to uncover all the things that you did well, such as any adlibs (like a good answer to a new question), or a new twist of phrase, or the way you emphasized a certain word. If a demonstration were especially effective, it would be worth embellishing it with new elements that will engage your audience even more. If you had a knockout example, you might want to take your time delivering it next time because you know that it is a real crowd-pleaser. If while reading your audience you observed moments when you piqued their interest, you will want to build on such moments for sure.

Self-assessment delivers shorter sales cycles and increased sales.

Since you know what it takes to create an environment to close, you have the ability to fix a problem. By constantly eliminating mistakes while building on all the things that work best, you will develop presentations that you can count on—every time. In other words, you get the consistency and predictability you need to reach your goals. This is the best confidence booster you can have.

When you have presentations that work flawlessly, you save a lot of energy, especially if you are giving dozens of informal presentations every day. If you work in an environment where customers drop in unannounced, you are always going to informally talk about your product offerings. By having proven presentations at your disposal, you can go on autopilot and discuss your products without having to think "presenting" it. While the information you are presenting looks and sounds informal to your customers, it is in fact deliberately structured, rehearsed and tested. This process better serves both you and your customers. You end up with more sales with less effort and your customers get the products and services they really need.

By now I would imagine that you are wondering, "Steven, you've told me what self-assessment is, why I need to do it and what to self-assess, but how do I self-assess?" Here's the answer. If a presentation does not work out for whatever reason, simply ask yourself this simple question: "Is it them or is it me?" Some people are often too quick to find fault in themselves, while others always assume that the problem is with the customer. The reality is that sometimes the problem lies with your customer and other times it is something that you did or did not do.

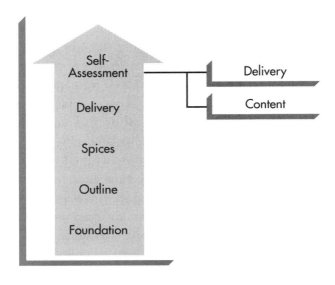

The source of the problem could be different with every presentation, so you have to specifically ask: "Is it them or is it me?" to get to the bottom of it. If the answer is, *"it is them,"* it might be that your audience was preoccupied with other matters. There might be internal politics in the way. You might be dealing with a consumer that is a chronic procrastinator or someone who is not ready, willing and able to make a decision. In short, it is beyond your control, in which case just move on and forget about it. On the other hand, if the answer to the question was *"you,"* then that is something which is entirely within your control to remedy.

With each presentation, you need to self-assess both the effectiveness of the content and your delivery of that content. Here's a simple scorecard to help you root-out any roadblocks to success. I urge you to use this tool after each presentation or sales call. I'll run through it quickly and give you a heads up on the kind of questions you should be asking yourself.

For content, rate *how effective your presentation was in meeting the objectives you set* in your Foundation section. Your objectives are the purest measurement of success. If you reach all your objectives, you did your job right. If you reach only some of them, then here is your opportunity to learn from experience and make the necessary enhancements. If you missed your objectives, identify the reasons why your objectives were not met. The more specific you can be, the more precise will be your remedy. Make a note of every corrective action you need to take. Do you know where I would look first? I'd check out how well I read my audience. If there was even one disconnect, chances are this was the beginning of the problem. If you find that you read the audience consistently and correctly, you'll have to dig further to see whether the issue was one of content or delivery.

SELF-ASSESSMENT SCORECARD

"5" is top score

CONTENT

	1	2	3	4	5
Meets Objectives:	1 ☐	2 ☐	3 ☐	4 ☐	5 ☐
Audience tuned in:	1 ☐	2 ☐	3 ☐	4 ☐	5 ☐
WANT TO listen:	1 ☐	2 ☐	3 ☐	4 ☐	5 ☐

Audience

	1	2	3	4	5
UNDERSTANDS:	1 ☐	2 ☐	3 ☐	4 ☐	5 ☐
Audience RELATES:	1 ☐	2 ☐	3 ☐	4 ☐	5 ☐
Participation:	1 ☐	2 ☐	3 ☐	4 ☐	5 ☐
Memorable:	1 ☐	2 ☐	3 ☐	4 ☐	5 ☐
Question Responses:	1 ☐	2 ☐	3 ☐	4 ☐	5 ☐
Objection Responses:	1 ☐	2 ☐	3 ☐	4 ☐	5 ☐

DELIVERY

Pacing — 1 ☐ 2 ☐ 3 ☐ 4 ☐ 5 ☐
Too slow/rushed   Good flow

Energy — 1 ☐ 2 ☐ 3 ☐ 4 ☐ 5 ☐
Low   High

Passion — 1 ☐ 2 ☐ 3 ☐ 4 ☐ 5 ☐
Reading   From the heart

Natural — 1 ☐ 2 ☐ 3 ☐ 4 ☐ 5 ☐
Stiff   Relaxed

Next, take a look at **whether your audience was tuned in**. Was the audience listening throughout? At what point did you lose your audience? (You might need to sharpen your skill at reading the audience.) What caused them to tune out? Was this an understanding issue or one of not relating? Do you need to move some content forward in your presentation? What steps can you take to prevent that from happening again?

Did your audience have to listen or did they WANT TO listen? Be honest. What measures did you take to make sure that your audience really wanted to listen? What engaged them the most? Did their body language indicate that they were highly motivated to listen? Were they asking questions? Were they asking questions that moved the conversation forward? Was your audience participating, and if so, were they eagerly participating or just going along with what everyone else was doing?

Did your audience UNDERSTAND everything? What signs did you pick up that told you they were confused in any way? If you did not read the audience correctly and did not pick up any clues, how can you double-up your efforts to read the audience more thoroughly the next time? If they did not UNDERSTAND something, what specifically did they not UNDERSTAND? How could this have been avoided? Would your meaning have been clearer if you used more examples or demonstrations?

Did your audience RELATE to your presentation? If not, do you need more examples or do your existing examples need to more accurately reflect the world of your audience? Do you need better metaphors or just more of them? Were you leveraging the words your audience wanted to hear? Were you involving your audience in your demonstrations? Could you have used better stories? Could the use of props be part of the remedy? Was your audience not participating, or if they were, should there have been more participation?

Speaking of participation, even if your audience could RELATE you might not have completely connected with them; it might have been a case of "You and Them" instead of the preferred state of "Us." So ***what was the quality of your audience participation?*** Were you asking enough questions? Did you engage the audience with questions that were interesting and intellectually stimulating? Did you encourage people to ask questions? Were people comfortable asking questions? Were there long gaps between those moments when the audience was participating? Did you give a demonstration without the active participation of the audience? Was everyone participating or only a few?

Also ask yourself: *how memorable was my presentation?* What did you do to make it memorable? What sort of comments did you get from people at the end of the presentation? What was the main point they took away? Was that the point you needed them to take away?

You know how important it is to build trust with effective answers to questions. *How effective were the responses to the questions you were asked?* Why were the questions being asked in the first place? Could you have prevented the need for them? Did you verify with the audience that your questions were satisfactory? Were there any questions you could not answer? If so, have you found the answers and got back to the person with the answers? How can you make your answers more effective? Do you need to do more research on a subject? Can you use any similes or metaphors to help people RELATE to your answers? Can props or visuals be helpful in making your answers more effective, engaging and memorable? Did you anticipate all the questions? If not, make sure to add the new questions in your Question Portfolio along with effective responses. If new questions were raised and you managed to adlib some terrific responses, make note of those responses too, and congratulations on a job well done!

How effective were your responses to objections raised? Had you anticipated them? What was the real reason behind the objections? If these were objections that you had anticipated, but did not have good responses, there is no time like the present to fine-tune them. But before you start rewriting, are you sure it was the approach that did not work or was it your delivery? If you weren't passionate, the big question is, *why?* Were you not focused on the value you bring to the table? Do you believe in what you are selling? Are you comfortable with your product knowledge? If the objections were new and you winged the responses, were you effective? If your responses were winners, write them down in your Objections Portfolio so you can leverage them the next time. If an unexpected objection came up and you need to work on a better response, create it now before the objection is raised again. If you already have a copy of *How To Make Hot Cold Calls,* open it up to the Objections Portfolio section where it provides you with a detailed process and examples for writing effective objection responses.

We touched on your delivery a moment ago, but let's look at it more thoroughly. Start with looking at your ***pacing***. Was it too slow? That depends on who your audience was. It might have been a good pace for you but it might have been slow for your audience, especially if most in the crowd were Type A personalities. If you were hurried, people might have missed and therefore misunderstood a key point. Your analytical types would have been in revolt because they want you to go slow and discuss all the details. If the pacing had a good flow, your audience would have been able to hear and digest every word. When your pacing is good it will be because your rehearsing paid off and you were comfortable delivering your material.

How was your ***energy?*** If it was low, what can you do to increase it the next time? Did the time of day have an effect? For example, if you presented after lunch, you might have been at high risk of dozing off because your body was diverting all its energy to digesting your food, especially those carbohydrates. And your audience might have been in the same boat. It might also be the dreaded 2:00 p.m. slot. If you are a morning person, your body clock will pack up for a snooze at 2:00, whether you like it or not. If I'm having a meeting or presentation at this time, I make sure to eat a light lunch. Your energy might also have been low because you were not prepared enough for your presentation or meeting. Did you take the time before the presentation to focus on the value you bring to the table? If your energy was high what did you do to motivate yourself before the presentation—to bring out your passion?

I couldn't have asked for a better segue. While you are checking into *passion*, ask yourself if you came across like you were reading your material or speaking from the heart. Even if you prepare notes, you don't have to sound like you are reading from them. Your evening news anchor-people read the news but you'd never know it by the way they speak to you. Speaking from the heart isn't about knowing your material off-by-heart, although that's always the preferred way to deliver your presentations. Speaking from the heart is about speaking passionately about everything, including how you answer questions. If you believe in what you are selling, and you love what you do, your passion should shine through. If you are not speaking passionately, it might be a focus issue. Did you take the time before your presentation to focus on the value of the opportunity you bring to the table? Did you visualize the presentation taking place? What can you add to your presentation to make it more interesting, fun or engaging for both you and your audience? Do you have a favorite part of your presentation that you look forward to? If you don't, that could be your problem right there. So create one. You'll be all the richer for it.

Speaking passionately is the ideal state of delivery. However, I would like to separate your passion from your ability to come across in a ***natural***, conversational manner. If you come across a little stiff, it could either be because you are not comfortable with your material, or there was a lack of preparation, or both. Is your product knowledge second to none? Have you given yourself plenty of rehearsal time? Do you have butterflies before you present? If so, apply what I recommended earlier to remedy this situation. If you managed to be totally relaxed, what did you do to get there? Was it your preparation? Was it your expert knowledge of the subject or your audience? Is it technique or just your natural disposition? If you did anything special, make note of it and apply it in your next presentation.

As you can see, your self-assessment enables you to build on past successes by reapplying all the things you did well. It also enables you to identify the root cause of any roadblocks to a successful presentation, and remedy problems so they do not surface again. When this process is repeated consistently (that's the magic word), then in a very short period of time, you will have tested and perfected each of your presentations to the point where you will know, with one hundred per cent certainty, that your audience will WANT TO listen and take action.

Self-assessment is just too good to restrict to presentations. You should be self-assessing after every sales call. When your sales call is amazing, make note of all the things you did to make it successful. On the other hand, if you walk out of a meeting and you did not get permission to go to the next step, you now know the question: "Is it them or is it me?" If it was "you," review each Island of Structure to measure how well you connected with your audience and look for any disconnects. For example, did you set the agenda? How thoroughly did you qualify the audience? Was the customer need clearly articulated and agreed to? Was there a sense of urgency? Was there anything your audience did not UNDERSTAND or RELATE to? Did you read your audience and observe any signs that they were tuning out? Did you pick up on the buying signals? Were the questions moving the conversation forward or backward? Did your audience give you any indication after the meeting as to how your discussion met their expectations?

In the event that you did not close on your last sales call, let's fix the problem right now. There is no time like the present.

Was it them or was it you?   ❑ Them ❑ Me

If it was "you," where/when did you disconnect from the audience?

. . . .
. . . .

What steps will you take to prevent this from recurring?

. . . .
. . . .
. . . .

How will you reward yourself for learning from your mistakes?

. . . .
. . . .
. . . .

When you get into the habit of self-assessing like this, you will stop making the same mistakes, and when that happens, your results will rise like helium.

Final Thoughts

Thank you for letting me share my experiences with you. All I've really done, though, is given you a canvas on which to paint your own experience and build your own Islands of Structure. You are well on your way to creating the environment where people will WANT TO buy. It's all rather intuitive when you think about it. Just find out what's important to people. Then help them with what they need. Be prepared, be clear in your meaning so that your audience will UNDERSTAND and RELATE, stay connected at all times, self-assess to learn from every experience, and rehearse, rehearse, rehearse.

You know, deep down, I've always relished the process of tracking down opportunities. I'm not sure if it's the thrill of discovery or the sense of accomplishment from the act of making something happen. All I know is that sales is an honorable profession, and one we all try hard to succeed in.

It's a feeling reinforced by a quote from a very successful intermediary named Mark Borkowski, President of Mercantile Mergers & Acquisitions in Toronto, who talks of sales as a place of honor. In Mark's words, "We are not always successful at sales, but salespeople we remain. And therein lies the excitement, the thrill and the privilege of what we do. We know the single-minded pursuit of our goals — sometimes lasting months - even years — in which our senses and instincts and reason are stretched to a wire-like keenness, while our opportunity — our one shot — draws slowly ever closer to hand. And through it all we are sales professionals, steeped in knowledge and passion, ever testing each other, encouraging each other, ever eager for chase, and no more — never more — ashamed to be called by our proper name, and to take our fair share of the glory."

Happy sales.